M000297620

DIANA

THE VOICE OF CHANGE

by

STEWART PEARCE

Published by
Filament Publishing Ltd
16, Croydon Road, Beddington,
Surrey CR0 4PA
www.filamentpublishing.com
+44(0)20 86882598

Diana: The Voice of Change

© 2021 Stewart Pearce
Cover by Kerry Beall

The right to be recognised as the author of this work has
been asserted by Stewart Pearce in accordance with the
Designs and copyrights Act 1988 Section 77.

All rights reserved
No portion of this work my be copied without the prior
written permission of the publishers

Printed by Ingram Content Group

CONTENTS

PREFACE

by Debbie Frank

WAS THERE EVER A MORE luminous figure than Diana, Princess of Wales? She possessed so many qualities that touched the souls of billions of people. From her initial entrance into our lives as a tender bud, she captured our hearts at every unfurling petal of her own extraordinary and intense life.

We witnessed the impact of her startling presence, yet this was never the kind of stardom that can be generated by flash-bulbs and crowds alone. It was the opposite of that—Diana's capacity to illuminate lives stemmed from her unique ability to be present to us, to give of herself, to bring herself whole-heartedly to us, wherever she was. We saw her flower from a young girl of 19, through the many frosts and hailstorms she endured, to become the radiant divinely feminine woman of her final years.

I was also present for Diana as her confidante and personal astrologer from February 1989 until her tragic, untimely death, and therefore saw the 'real' Diana move through all her stages of initiation, to become the most extraordinary woman. Our final meeting, just one month before she died will always remain in my memory, for she had reached a scale of luminosity I had never seen before.

How did this happen? Diana knew she was on a journey of personal empowerment, of spiritual development, and she actively sought out those special mentors and teachers of light who could help her fulfill that destiny. It is no co-incidence, that she reached the pinnacle of her personal power in the last two years before her death as she invited the most divinely inspired guide, the remarkable Stewart Pearce, to birth her into becoming the Voice of Change. Stewart has a pure and direct link to the Angels (of which Diana is now one) and has affected so much powerful change through the element of the divine feminine in our lives, through many of the female leaders of today. He has vast reservoirs of wisdom to impart, and is an earth angel himself, who is inspired to help women become their true selves. His spiritual guidance of Diana was a great catalyst in her life, as she emerged into her full glory.

As she explored and discovered the means by which she could pour her divine feminine wisdom into the world through her voice and presence, she literally blossomed before our eyes. There was a magnified radiance about her, so that she emerged from her divorce in 1996 as a woman who had faced the stern stonewalling of the patriarchy and had come through with the grace of both her vulnerability and power intact.

Through Stewart's extraordinary work with Diana, her message of love and healing of the heart can now be channeled into your own life. This is what Diana would have wanted. It is a gift that is sent to you with her love. Diana's love is one that keeps on giving, and giving, and we are blessed to be given access to Stewarts's unique transformational breath-work, finding of our own unique signature sound, heavenly mantras and divine sacramental codes. The very same work that Diana gained from Stewart, and then internalized to up-level her engagement with the divine feminine force, is now your very own workbook.

At this profound and pivotal point in our history, as the old establishment is being challenged by voices of change on every level, we are being urged to unite in speaking our truth and living it. We are all born with our own special note that is a unique blend of our breath, our voice, and our soulful being. However, some of us never find this note, or the courage to voice it to the outside world.

It is Stewart's life-long engagement with voice, resonance and frequency that fascinated Diana, and she not only found her note through Stewart's coaching, but also spoke her message to the world straight from her heart. The depth and scale of Diana's note spoke volumes and permeated the walls of the patriarchy, leading to the abolition of landmines, the transformation of the Royal Family, and the legacy of love that she left as the powerful voice of the divine feminine.

It is time for us all to find our note, our voice, and speak out, as Stewart suggests it can be so. Within the pages of his book you will discover this. Delight in it, and your pathway to empowerment will constellate. The world needs to hear what you long to say, and these words from your heart will join in the song of the Divine Feminine that raises the entire frequency of the planet.

With love and blessings

Debbie Frank
Astrologer and Life Healer

www.debbiefrankastrology.com

ACKNOWLEDGEMENTS

Writing and publishing books is a co-creative experience, and from the deeper recesses of my soul, I thank the dear ones who have kept me balanced through their complete belief in my writing, my contribution, my craft, and my mystical nature. You who made me laugh as I grappled with the words that poured from me, please continue blessing me with your love, and I hope my choices are the best, in complete loving service to the wondrous lady who lives at the very core of the book!

Many heartfelt thanks to the pioneering glory of my Literary Agent - Susan Mears - who indefatigably presented the book's essence to publisher after publisher, even though the majority showed they were palpably disinterested. To this day we still do not know why they couldn't support the soul, the beauty and the grace of dear Diana the exemplar of love. Yet by reading the contents, I pray that all who venture here send beautiful prayers, that hardened hearts and mean minds be healed, transformed, and moved to love!

Huge gratitude goes to Katie Rose for her warm support and tireless editorship, and to Ranchor Prime for giving life to the work, which I passionately believe in, thank you, thank you, thank you.

Then there was my beautiful artist Kerry Beall, who came to me out of the blue when I most needed her. I had been searching for a gifted artist as refined and talented as she is, with an open heart and a crafty style, who was in sympathetic alignment with the global arousal of the Divine Feminine. When I first commissioned Kerry and saw the Diana Portrait she painted for me I wept, for I knew she was seeing Diana as she is now. I hold immense gratitude to Kerry's amazing creative talent, and the wonder of who she is!

Lastly to the readers and supporters of my work, it is for you that I write. My love and thanks are more boundless than the sea, my hope is rich that you enjoy these contents, and my soul is made joyous by the tenderness and curiosity of your passionate interest. I hope and pray I never let you down!

Love & Light
Stewart
January 2020

INTRODUCTION

'I knew something profound was coming my way.'
DIANA, PRINCESS OF WALES

THIS BOOK IS A CALL TO ACTION for women everywhere, for it begins and ends with love. The essence of this book urges the heart of each woman to awaken and rise up, to heal any breakage within, and to commit to a flow of empathy, as an opening impulse for the mighty voice of change. Indeed, it was Diana's greatest desire that through her example each woman of the world would find their own authentic voice, fulfilling their unique purpose, and liberating love to transcend any enmity. Diana believed that wherever tyranny was it would be freed by grace, that wherever cruelty existed it would be freed by bravery, and that wherever the voice of oppression occurred it would be freed by the voice of kindness. In this, Diana was a trailblazer!

Her starry light illuminates the conviction of women everywhere, and as conviction is a force multiplier, women today are mustering their own power in order to claim sovereignty, liberating themselves from the specter of masculine supremacy, evoking gender equality, evolving emotional transparency, and fostering integrity in a multitude of ways. The women of the world are inspiring initiatives that arose from Diana's aspirations, and therefore lead us all to contemplate each other with compassion, creating unity consciousness, and espousing that all men and women be created equal for life, liberty, and the pursuit of happiness.

In this Diana was a figurehead, and so her incredible story is fit for retelling now, yet through a different lens from before. For Diana's voice embodied the zeitgeist of the 1980-90s which led to powerful reforms within the monarchy, giving rise to a redefinition of personal sovereignty. Within the wake of Diana's universal and inspirational appeal, her contribution rests as bedrock for the growing movements of #METOOCAMPAIGN, #TIMESUP, #WHYDIDN'TIREPORT, and #TRANSLIVESMATTER, as well being a force of inspiration for the many charities she supported.

Echoing this Diana's two sons broadcast her legacy through their own extraordinary work, through mindful living processes, and various charities. For example, Harry founded 'Sentabale' in order to support the wellbeing of young people affected by the HIV Virus living in Lesotho and Botswana. He also brought about constitutional revolution by marrying a Black American actress divorcee, and has pioneered programs concerned with mindfulness awareness, particularly through the 'Heads Together' campaign. Whilst, brother William tends to his young family and initiates cultural amelioration through his own charity work concerning Wild Life Conservation and Cyber Bullying.

All this occurs because Diana led the way. Diana brought credence to a new form of authenticity, inclusivity, and transparency. Diana embodied a crucible of human virtue from which poured forth—joy, freedom, truth, empathy, compassion, inclusivity, forgiveness, charity, and love. These virtues she illuminated as a reminder for us all, that these feeling states bring us back to harmony, giving us strength to wring purpose from change. Thereby Diana's heartfelt virtues exist like lifebuoys in any troubled ocean for they give us hope and strength to endure, knowing that we will always be loved by the people who care, by the Universe which gives us life, and by the Divine intelligence that gathers in the creation of each sentient being.

'A woman will be trapped in emotional bondage, so long as she worries that she has to make a choice between being heard and being loved!'
STEWART PEARCE

Diana gave permission for the formal behavior that stultifies love, to be reinvented, for emotional aloofness to be made transparent, for starched stuffiness to be given a human face, for feeling expression to be given its rightful place, and for dismissive criticism to be turned into discerning care. Indeed, viewing Diana's life through the lens of the last twenty-two years, we can see what a truly extraordinary story hers was, and how her memory lives on in people's hearts, still bringing joy and tenderness to all our lives today. Each climax and nadir of her extraordinary story appears to have been crafted by the sage-writer of an ancient Greek drama. Within this book we will explore the full significance of this extraordinary person and how her personal odyssey—the sojourn of the heroine's quest—was wrought by archetypal significance!

The Queen of Everyone's Heart

'I'd like to be a queen of people's hearts, but I don't see myself being queen of this country.'
Diana

No one in history has been so universally adored as Diana Princess of Wales. Never before has a public figure so deeply affected the people of the world, as Diana did. Not even the most celebrated screen actress or celebrity icon has been photographed as much as Diana. The Queen of Everyone's hearts was captivating, inspiring, alluring, charismatic, and through her innate power influenced even the most diehard cynic with her warmth, beauty, love, and kindness. It was as though she had touched not just everyone's hand but had permeated deep into their soul with her radiant love, with her incandescent grace, which were known to melt grown men's bones.

Amongst strong men she would walk, with Presidents and Prime Ministers she would talk, yet many could make little sense of what was happening to them. For wherever Diana moved a wave of grace passed through everyone, shifting each person into richer contact with their inner essence or higher self, moving everyone into the heart-felt soul of empathy and compassion.

But, within the British Royal Family Diana experienced opposition, for she established a new way of being that contradicted the protocols of tradition and the social rubrics that had existed for over a hundred years. It was through these social boundaries that feelings were withheld, personal emotions often stifled, and significant issues rarely personalized. Instead, Diana's way was to overtly express what she felt, and after developing the courage of her first ten years as a Royal personage she confessed:

> 'I do things differently, for I rule from the heart, not from the head.'

This observation became her lodestone, her brand signature, her USP, and as she spoke to us all through her actions, she also encouraged us to open our hearts, to unleash kindness, express love, and unbridle our compassion. For

Diana showed her vulnerability in public, meeting people face on, and holding their hands with such care, and without gloves. But this behavior was considered totally inappropriate by other members of the Windsor Family. For they did what they had always done, remaining aloof to the collective feeling, withholding their emotions, hiding behind the royal veneer, and remaining 'stoic' in order to create their own brand of mystique.

In counterpoise, Diana attended engagements with her astonishing blue eyes brimming with kindness, freshening the nature of formality by creating witty, joyous, naughtiness, with a familiarity that always wooed the crowds, but was criticized by the family she had married into. Indeed, when she described their disapproval of her process during a TV program in 1995 Diana confessed: *'There is no better way to dismantle a personality than to isolate it!'* and this they did through not fully understanding Diana's predicament.

Even so, it is uplifting to reflect on the courage and daring that Diana possessed as the change-maker she was, particularly during the latter part of her life. She spoke the truth as she felt it, she was endearing when sensing someone's frailty, she loved where love was absent, and she bestowed generosity in order to create parity.

Yet in contrast, during the early years when the royals disparaged her fragility, Diana hid within her Bulimia, and became bound by victim consciousness. When they criticized her playfulness, she crumbled into silence, when they chastised her difference of opinion she dissolved into tears. Until, that is, she began to acquire the ability to transform the crippling negativity, by searching for her own power, her own voice, her own credibility. Then, as epiphany dawned, Diana discovered a unique vocal timbre, with a voice that was unmistakably the call of the heart, pregnant with truth, yearning for the magic of synergy, searching for kindness in the eyes of those before her, and rich with a desire to make empathic connection.

The Voice Of Change Manifesto

Are you full-lunged and limber-lipped from long trial?
From vigorous practice? From physique?
Do you move in those broad lands as broad as they?
Come duly to the divine power to speak words?
For only at last after many years, after chastity, friendship,
procreation, prudence, nakedness,
After treading ground and breasting river and lake,
After a loosened throat, after absorbing eras, temperaments, races,
After knowledge, freedom, crimes,
After complete faith, after clarifyings, elevations
and removing obstructions,
After these and more, it is just possible that there comes to a
man, a woman, the divine power to speak words;
Then toward that man or woman swiftly hasten all—
none refuse, all attend.'
Walt Whitman

Diana introduced us to the voice of change as the voice of love, which became the voice of the heart balancing out the excesses of the cerebral mind, rigid with its own controls. Diana believed that:

The voice of change holds sparkling authenticity in the waves of its resonance. The voice of change speaks with a passionate truth as it is one of the most powerful tools we humans possess. The voice of change does not hide from fear, humiliation, embarrassment, or subterfuge. The voice of change lives joyously, freely, empowering our identity into creation. The voice of change speaks, shouts, cries-out with a gusto that evolves courage and determination, finding all of its breath-ways to express personal sovereignty. The voice of change sounds our world into existence. The voice of change does not mumble or murmur, it resonates with a force that arises from deep inside, accumulated through years of plummeting the deep pools of our consciousness, and expressing the conviction that lies within—a truth which is most credible, most raw, most vital, and most beautiful—about who we are, and how our soul breathes.

The voice of change is fully owned by the speaker, physically resonating from their core, clarified by distinct diction, reverberating its primal sound, honed by the beauty of its physical capacity, and crafted by the majesty of its mental clarity. The voice of change is shaped by bare survival, identifying and then resolving pain, ignominy, strife, abuse, denial, guilt, shame, injustice, betrayal, and hatred. The voice of change allows the soul of the speaker to shape the destiny of their message, and thus claims a position of unique brilliance. The voice of change has only one clear quest—to follow the path of destiny, and that it be laid with silver and gold—leading the individual to an open heart, and a creative excellence that is full of the loving force of the Universe!

The voice of change is the only constant we have. For in truth, when change occurs it signifies that we are fully alive, moving forward, spiriting ourselves into creation, aligning our soul's destiny, dynamically engaged, moving to the beat of our hearts, breathing to the steadiness of our footfall, walking with courageous gravity along the red path of life.

A WOMAN'S WITNESS

'I think every strong woman in history has had to walk
a similar path, and I think it is her strength that causes the
confusion and the fear.
Why is she strong? Where does she get it from?
Where is she taking it?
Where is she going to use it?
Why do the public still support her?
When I say public, I mean that when I do an engagement
there are a great many people there.'
DIANA

Diana's voice appears within a chronicle that records many other outstanding female voices, and as her role became clear she personally identified with many of these voices that echo within the history books. Voices such as Emmeline Pankhurst, Rosa Parks, Benazir Bhutto, Mo Mowlem, Anita Roddick, Maya Angelou, and today Gloria Steinem, Nina Simone, Oprah Winfrey, Marianne Williamson, Michelle Obama, and Chimananda Nigozi Adhici. All are groundbreaking, and many have grown through the craft of voice coaching.

Change is mighty at present, for in September 2018, one of the most crucial gender evaluations occurred in our twenty-first century, during the week of the FORD VS. KAVANAUGH US Senate Judiciary Committee Hearing. This process saw Dr. Christine Blasey Ford raise her right hand, and swear to tell the truth, the whole truth and nothing but the truth. Yet it was clear from that moment onwards that this unassuming psychology professor, the mother of two children, was to change the course of history in real time.

Dr Ford alleged she had been the victim of sexual assault perpetrated by Brett Kavanaugh 36 years earlier. But when Dr Ford spoke her testimony, she was side-railed by the Senate Committee, even though belief in her veracity had been well established. From the opening of Dr Ford's statement: *'I'm here today not because I want to be, I'm actually terrified, but I felt it my civic duty!'* the American public watched with their mouths agape and voted that 85% of her statement was true. When the hearing reached its ghastly completion, Dr Ford had done much more than prove herself a credible witness!

For millions of women and men around the Globe who had sat pinned to their Tablets or their TV's, Christine had outshone Kavanaugh as the leading protagonist in the whole complex drama. Yet what Dr Ford did was to inspire women around the world to call in to C-SPAN, CNN and FOX NEWS, to tell their own decades-old stories about sexual harassment, rape and inequality. The hash tags #metoo and #whyididn'treport literally exploded forth on social media, with a hugely supportive cry from those people who had never been public about the sexual assault they had also been victim to. People from Albuquerque to Zanzibar watched this testimony, some gathering in disbelief around their tablets and smart phones, some with horror in mind, some with empathic hands held over their hearts, and most with mouths agape as they listened in shock.

Just so, Diana startled the world when she faced the incredulity of her own husband's infidelity. It is true this action wasn't a physical assault as in the case of Dr Ford, yet still it amounted to psychic or psychological wounding, persistently driven home not just by her husband, but also by many of his austere supporters. You see the Royal Household had perceived Diana as 'loony', and similarly at times the daily tabloids became cruelly dismissive of her via statements like: 'Do we need this heroine of the people?' whilst ravenously chasing her for the next lurid picture of her face, a body, or her breasts. I was with her on two occasions when members of the press bitterly swore at her, simply to trigger a response. Incontrovertibly the answer that came back from the people was unequivocal: *Yes, Diana is the love and compassion that will bring about the democratization of the monarchy.*

THE ROLE OF DIANA'S COACH

Through the latter part of 1995 to her untimely death in 1997 I took a giant intake of breath and became the voice, presentation and life coach to the Princess. My role was to enhance Diana's presence in the world, in a field of action that included her charitable work, and all the concerns that were her keen interest. Although Diana was the most celebrated woman, it was also essential for her to develop a voice craft which in turn would help her to create greater confidence, persona, passion, persuasion, and physical presence, in order to communicate her newly empowered role with greater gravitas, presence and magic. For her to find her sovereignty!

Our mutual agreement was that the work would be protected by confidentiality, and therefore very few people knew—until now that is—because now the times have radically changed, and the women of the world are roused. Now it is time for an out breath to take place, so that I may inspire other women in the same way that I helped Diana bring forth her voice of change.

The request to consult with the Princess came to me just as the Martin Bashir Panorama interview was broadcast in 1995, which was subsequently viewed by 22.8 million viewers. Frankly I had huge reservations about becoming involved, not because I wasn't honored by the commission, but because I couldn't vision how I could be part of the 'circus' that surrounded Diana. The notoriety that moved with the Princess was crazily orchestrated by the 'paparazzi', and I was made keenly aware of the fact that a number of her leading advisors, therapists, and consultants, had treacherously sold their indiscretions to the tabloids for vast personal profit. This produced an understandable sense of betrayal in Diana—a wound like a deep gash—and so I insisted that our consultations be underscored by complete confidentiality.

Of course, at the same time I felt a great honor to be asked, and from the moment I met Diana, over lunch at the famed restaurant San Lorenzo in London's Knightsbridge, I felt a deep love and respect for her, and for Mara Berni who had introduced us. Mara had been the guiding force within so many people's lives from the 1960's to her death in 2012, which all occurred from her legendary restaurant in Beauchamp Place. It was well known that all Mara needed was a telephone call from Mick Jagger in the late 1960's, and she would make space for the Rolling Stones to arrive in the early hours of the morning, post-concert, to be fed her extraordinary Pasta and Sauces.

A DEDICATION TO LOVE

This book is a dedication to Diana's unique love, and so my writing does not include ridiculous disclosures, discredits, or hearsays that would trifle Diana's life or provide expositions of her innermost secrets. Rather this is an account that addresses the very essence of who and what Diana was and is, so that we may comprehend her true significance, and heal the lamentation of her passing, a profound sadness that still scores the hearts and souls of many. My wish is to reinterpret her glory, to take example from her unique experience, and so help to empower and inspire the women of the world.

We also need to celebrate the enormity of what Diana gave us, the gifts that provide reason for her extraordinary life and death. For her life was a cipher by which the women of the world can also be read. Therefore, you may want to ask these candid questions—

1. Who was Diana, in the sense of where did her energy arise from?
2. Was her position in the royal family significant to their lives at a time when the monarchy was seen to be unnecessary?
3. What was her extraordinary public appeal based on?
4. Was her death a ritual killing, or an archetypal sacrifice?
5. Why was she taken from us?
6. Will Diana's memory ever fade?
7. What was the phenomenon that took place at her death which affected us all, changing billions of people's lives?
8. Will the vital qualities of her being, her compassion, kindness and immediacy, assist the people of the

world to uplift themselves into positions of even greater emotional truth and intelligence?

9. Will Diana's presence be further realized through knowing that love is the purest factor in all our lives?

10. What contribution can the life of Diana provide to our lives, in this seething world of Trump and Brexit?

11. What is Diana now?

12. Where is she?—as so many people feel her to be immensely close to them

All these questions and many others are the substance of my account, and so I aim to answer the answerable and question the unquestionable!

What This Book Will Hold For You

The objective of this book explains how Diana physically and psychologically became the radiant, and uplifted being that she was. How by using her voice she discovered a richer life, so that she could amplify her promise to augment world change. Indeed, through the exercises of this book you will find a way of expanding your own voice just as Diana did. The result of which will move you into greater harmony, saturating your whole being with a confidence that will amplify your life experience, bringing you greater untold joy.

The promise of the book is that it's packed with useful

tips and techniques of how to truly be you, with that special touch that Diana had. Within these pages there are countless ways of becoming an instrument of power and peace in your own life, that will stimulate and evoke your personal presence, persuasive magnetism, gracious charisma, and creative excellence. All these processes will help you attain the greatest vision of you!

The value of the book provides a means by which the challenges of life can be alchemically transformed, so that the multitude of pain that you may amass can be transmuted. All the major processes I used with Diana to elicit freedom are here for you to use, for she gave me permission to share these with you at a date when they would be necessary, and these processes furthermore will become known as THE DIANA HEART PATH.

My heart's desire is to enchant, uplift, inspire, reassure, and genuinely aid you towards transcendence. And so within this book there are many strategic ways of being, life enhancing meditations, shimmering affirmations, and relaxing processes that Diana directly experienced, and which we also want to gift you, to encourage your own journey towards empowerment and enlightenment.

Chapter 1   TO CATCH A FALLING STAR—we will reflect on Diana's archetypal story

Chapter 2   THE VOICE OF CHANGE—we will explore 7 vocal processes Diana used

Chapter 3   THE ANOINTED ONE—we will follow the opening of Diana's journey through 3 Guardian Measures, and 7 Inspirational Sacraments.

Perhaps this is a good point in your reading to ask yourself what it is that you wish the book to provide you? Because although Diana evidently had immense value as an icon, she was also a lady of the people, and her emphasis was placed upon truly and compassionately helping anyone in difficulty. So, if you are reaching for this book during a period of such challenge, that racks your existence or troubles you deeply, Diana wants to help you, just as she did when she was alive. If you are at the height of your powers, and life is thrilling, and thriving beautifully, Diana wants you to celebrate with her the victory of your success!

Questions you might want to ask are:

How will this book benefit me, and what will I gain?

What key skills do I want to encounter as I read it?

How will the exercises in this book make me feel?

Will my memory of Diana be enhanced?

How can I become closer to her, and her unique Heart Path?

Will this mean that I will be a better and more mature person?

May the book teach me ways of improving my inter-personal communications?

Can I learn how to be honest without hurting people's feelings?

Will the book open ideas to help me find my own life purpose?

Will Diana's life illuminate a way of healing my own challenges?

Does Diana still express her love from a repositioning of her spirit?

Can I banish my hate by reading about Diana's love?

HOW TO LIVE THE RADIANCE OF DIANA

Diana wanted the qualities she possessed to be yours, so that the empowerment processes and points of transformation which helped her develop the confidence that produced the allure you so admired, could be yours also, and after just a little application!

By sharing our work together, I want you to claim the power of the Voice of Change for yourself. Then you will become the vessel through which the efficacy of this work has true affect. All the substance that is addressed within the book is approached in easy and endearing terms, just as Diana would have it, so there is nothing starchy or distant or superior about the work. Rather it provides a host of possibilities based on the self-love that will bring you abundant riches!

If you are searching for your soul's purpose, this work will gently lead you to a more than satisfactory conclusion, the fulfillment of your life's dream. If you are hurting, this work will help you heal. If you feel disorientated or lost, this work will lead you home. If you are feeling confused about your values, this work will give you definition. If you feel dismayed by the world's current dysfunction, this work will appear like a lighthouse in an ocean of chaos. Just read on and feel Diana's love permeating throughout these words, moving you into a vastly better place than when you first began to search, for you will feel Diana's sweetness filling your heart and soul!

A PATH OF ENLIGHTENMENT

Diana wanted you to feel that you are loved, that you are comforted, that you are secure, and that when you feel this love you will also find your purpose is to love in like measure, starting with yourself. Diana believed that if we are filled with love, a power arises within us to create a life of infinite possibility. And Diana showed by example, for she believed that within our being is a love that can direct you to think and feel in ways that reflect and attract all the love that you want. This type of thinking and feeling is called ENLIGHTENMENT, and this state of being defines a choice that is available to you in every moment.

We live in such turbulent times, and it is easy to feel our internal value system askew. It's easy to feel dislodged when all our values barrack against each other, arguing about which way we should view right and wrong, good or bad, just and unjust, fair or rude. Often, we abandon our own value system under the weight of the rules the world gives us. Then a gulf emerges between what feels right within and what is real without. The elements of affection and sharing used at home become distorted by the uncaring nature of the world. The common good we feel within our family or with intimate friends who give us safety and comfort, is replaced by a rapacious desire to personally succeed. This egocentric behavior drives us to elbow people out of the way, rather than to step aside in grace. Then sooner or later we realize life is full of rushing, competing our way to the finishing line, and just like the horizon, the finishing line keeps moving further and further away!

Always remember, Diana journeyed into the pit of her own despair for some time, like many of us do, just as you might be doing right now. But then she steadily climbed to a new way of being, that allowed her light to shine more brightly, with a self-love that encouraged many to feel the same. Diana stopped thinking of herself as a random piece of flotsam and jetsam, living within a cruel universe that didn't care. She turned all the limiting beliefs that once held her prisoner, into a creation of pure wonder and magic. For she found that, if she believed in herself to be the effect of a loving world, her light would shine in a special way, like a beacon of compassion that made miracles happen. Whereas if she thought 'victim thoughts' she fell foul to challenging situations which debilitated her, bringing the demons of fear, denial, guilt and shame to the fore. Diana may have been victimized, but she rarely saw herself as a victim, so her light became not just an attainment, but a true delight!

ENLIGHTENMENT is the answer to every horrible situation in life. If you can readjust your thinking to realize that within each situation that may have control over you, within every experience that gives rise to the feeling that you are merely the effect of an angry cause, within every drama where you feel fear, your soul is beckoning you to know that the Divine lives within you, and there is no force that the Divine cannot manage. There are no mortal situations where you are powerless, if you believe in a higher power!

Instead, pause, detach, feel stillness and note that whenever your essence is obscured by the cantankerous nature of the world, you may also think another thought, and so remember that the Divinity in the Universe gave birth to you. The Universe is similarly designed to uplift you, moving you back into a state of natural innocence, wonder, joy and freedom. And when you remember that the Universe is a personal love letter written to you by the Divine, the world will appear to be rich and abundant!

Diana believed that she was an expression of Divine perfection, and that the majesty of the universe, was an implicit force organized and aligned by the intelligence of the Source for all sentient beings. She felt that from spiritual essence arose all material manifestation, and that this was the distinguishing principle of the Universe. Just consider for a moment that the law of gravity isn't just a belief, but a truth. Can you see that this is true, whether you believe it or not?

You see, Diana realized that all spiritual values are a modus operandi, designed to help us live our consciousness out loud, living lives that express greatness, goodness, and generosity. One of the truly magnificent spiritual teachers of these principles is Marianne Williamson, and Diana loved her teachings, so here is one of Marianne's significant poems:

'Our deepest fear is not that we are inadequate.
Our deepest fear is that we are powerful beyond measure.
It is our light, not our darkness that most frightens us.
We ask ourselves, who am I to be brilliant, gorgeous,
talented, fabulous?
Actually, who are you not to be? You are a child of God.
You're playing small does not serve the world.
There is nothing enlightened about shrinking so that
other people won't feel insecure around you.
We are all meant to shine, as children do.
We were born to make manifest the glory of God that
is within us.
It's not just in some of us; it's in everyone.
And as we let our own light shine,
We unconsciously give other people permission to
do the same.
As we are liberated from our own fear,
Our presence automatically liberates others.'
MARIANNE WILLIAMSON
From 'A Return To Love'

THE CALL OF THE HEART

'HIV doesn't make people dangerous to know, so you can
shake their hands and give them a hug.
Heaven knows they need it.'
DIANA

At the time of her tragic death, Diana the People's Princess had become the Queen of Everybody's Heart. Whereas now, the instrument of her unique love, the tenderness of her heartfelt compassion, the definition of her role as an Ambassador for Peace, all and more are details that elevate our consciousness as we review her life. When Diana made the decision to shake the hands of the Aids patients she met without gloves, she shook the world into a new reality! And it is this reality that shakes us now, as each of us has our own part to play, and nothing is expected or required of us that we don't already have to give. As Diana showed we are all needed, we all have our own unique gifts and qualities, we all know what our destinies can be. If we can just give ourselves time to be still, and feel within what Diana was all about, then it will be our hearts that will define our own specific calling!

Some of you will educate, some will learn, some of you will feel politically active, and some will make dinner. Some of you will be compassionate to the poor, and some will legislate social change. Some of you will make babies, and some will create other projects. And just as Diana did, some of you may anonymously visit people in hospital, or sit with those who are lonely, unwell, or lost, and bring comfort.

The Diana Heart Path will give you the inspiration to see what you can do to fashion your own charity, and so please do click on the website when you get a moment.

As Diana said:

'I can't be indifferent to those who suffer or need care. I can't ignore social unfairness or injustice. I can't turn a blind eye to the homeless. We must believe that our voices and actions will change the world, and then find a way of speaking forth about the change that is needed—this is our moral imperative!'

Enjoy the read!

CHAPTER ONE

TO CATCH A FALLING STAR

THE STORY OF A SHINING ONE

'We are precious, make no mistake, and each one of us is destined to live that special force. We are magnificent human beings who have been given an almighty gift—the ability to create our own lives without limitation. Then along comes an anointed one, who given the chance shines as brightly as the pole star. These are the shining ones who lead the way, and Diana was such a one!'
OPRAH WINFREY

WHAT YOU ARE ABOUT TO READ is a first-time revelation. What you will see before you will be the true meaning behind the life and death of the extraordinary Diana. What you will feel will be an immense empathy, and the triumph that helped her soar through a journey from victim to victor.

Yet there is a caveat, for what I offer here is not a 'kiss and tell' account of Diana's temperament or shadow. Rather you will read a record of how Diana realized her soul potential, how she moved deeply into the essence of being her own self, into the profound love that lay within her soul, and whilst there how she identified the conflicts, beginning the rite of transmutation for each challenge. This allowed her to become the incandescent star that illuminated both the earth and skies.

Diana expressed this light through her beauty, care, love, compassion, joy, fun, flair, and her courageous will to breathe afresh. For these were the vital assets of her extraordinary being, our Diana, our Queen of Hearts, our beautiful Star, our exemplar of love. This was the young woman who astonished the whole world by her honesty and set about alleviating the suffering of other sentient beings, whilst she incontrovertibly changed the nature of the British monarchy, and the function of establishment!

Through the perspective of the last twenty-two years we may review the life of Diana from the many biographies that have been written about her, yet my belief is that they exist as incomplete chronicles, for they comment on the events Diana attended, and what opinions many had of her as though they were Court Diaries, or critical Diarists of a bygone age. I believe that by moving deeper, moving into the very meaning of her existence, moving to the level of causation, that we will find the essence of Diana, and the crucial consequences of her personal impact on global events. Once there, seeping in the soul of this extraordinary human being, you will truly learn the value of her existence as much as these pages may reveal, and why her life was so precipitous pitching between personal conflict and public adulation.

From the revelation of this account you will see how you can reinterpret the wonder and magic that was Diana. What her dreams were, what her principle interests were, what her major growth spurts were, how she processed raw challenge, how and what she needed to heal, how she managed her immense love and developed boundaries, how she rose above the rank criticism within the family that she represented, how important it was for her to have the sons she had, and how at the same time she evolved into her own distinct radiance, and in effect becoming a world superpower.

Through reading this account you will reinterpret the story of Diana's life. You will find ways to question the unquestionable, answer the unanswerable, and believe in the unbelievable. You will examine the real cause of Diana's odyssey and not just the effects of her epic story. And so, what you will read is by no means a superficial account, for whatever we saw happening before us as the story of Diana's personality emerged, we also saw her personal circumstances eventually precipitate a seismic shift in global consciousness.

Through the rise and fall of Diana's Star, millions and millions of people were moved to love, to heal, to transform the misspent tears and loss of love for their own Mothers, Sisters, Daughters, Female friends or Lovers, including the otherworldly supernatural force of the Divine Mother. My belief is that the seismic nature of Diana's quest was brought about by the marriage of her belief in love, the liberation of her loving, her total belief in spirit, and the hand of destiny—those unseen forces that permeate throughout all our lives, allowing us to be destined for ascendant glory, whilst others watch on and are influenced.

WHAT IS FATE?

In ancient times this force was believed to be FATE, represented in the form of three goddesses, who wove Life's Tapestry and organized the destinies of men and women. CLOTHO spun the thread, LACHESIS wove the thread into a life story, and ATROPOS cut the thread, thus ending the individual's life journey and soul destiny. In this context Diana's fate was set to illuminate the conviction of love, joy and charity as the great beacons of world saving. And in turn these forces ignite the archetypal constellations of human meaning and divine significance. We saw and felt this literally explode into our hearts during certain moments of her life, very particularly at her death. For these forces allowed us to see the star of her own divine degree, as a distinct and blessed soul quest.

I observed this closely during the last two years of Diana's life, and now my deepest desire is to evoke her force through these pages, so that you too may feel her presence in your mind, in your heart, and in your soul. Weaving the glory of your existence with hers is what she gave me permission to do, when the time was right. Diana wanted me to reveal why her destiny had been chosen, in subtle and palpable ways to be the phenomenon it was. Therefore, this book explores the reason for her 'becoming', how she ascended as a star of infinite renown, and how she impinged on all of our lives. This is what Diana wanted just for you!

In this first chapter will be revealed the key aspects of Diana that became the lodestones of her journey, the odyssey of the heroine. I will share with you the force that stirred within her, how she transformed, how she claimed her own voice, and how she became the voice of change which brought hope to many of the oppressed people of the world—the sick, the unloved, or the lost. How her voice soothed us, before calling out the treachery of the disdaining masculine which disparaged her. How she became a trailblazing presence that illuminated the conviction of every woman who wished to liberate herself from the prison of condemnation, from a state of victimhood.

We can see her presence shifting the consciousness of people still, through the changes that have taken place in attitude towards HIV, the Land Mines issue, the challenge of Mental Health, Meghan Markle's remarkable story, and the tremendous movements which have inspired individual women to join in the solidarity of unified purpose. The unseen force that was and is Diana awakens millions of women, and when illuminated in our hearts this force will help to shape our destiny, supporting us to grow and become the Voice of Change.

Step by step I want to show you how Diana was moved to claim her strength by eliciting the unique power of her voice, creating an inner harmony that in turn led her to define her personal sovereignty. For by literally embodying her voice she was able to express the disharmony and disorientation locked within, and then to transform pain into pleasure, victim into victor, striving into thriving. Being this meant Diana gained the courage to live her purpose, optimizing all that she believed in for the highest vision of herself, and from the essence of her core. In this sense the embodiment of her voice became of paramount importance to her, just as it can be for you, because sound is at the core of creation. Then as we move forward into the forthcoming chapters I will guide you through the unique physical empowerments, soul meditations, and vocal affirmations that Diana used. Together we will embark on the star-lit opportunity of THE DIANA HEART PATH process.

A BRIGHT STAR FALLS

'Twenty years ago, the world lost an angel'
ELTON JOHN

A bright star fell from heaven one August night in 1997. That event was beyond the extraordinary—it was an almost unbelievable catastrophe.

On the morning of August 31st 1997, wherever you were, whatever time you woke, or however your values were positioned, you would have opened your eyes to a vastly different world from the one you fell asleep to. This new world held a terrible mystery arising from a shooting star passing over your sleeping head, and exploding against the thirteenth pillar of the Pont de L'Alma traffic tunnel in Paris. When the people of the United Kingdom opened their eyes that quiet Sunday morning, they found their favorite Princess dead, and in lamentation asked—'how could this have come to pass, was this a planned killing—was this meant to happen, or was this just an horrific accident?' The world was simply shocked out of consciousness.

From another point of focus, the citizens of North America had spent the whole night in historic vigil. For during that August 30th evening TV program viewing was dramatically interrupted by a newsflash, detailing Diana and Dodi's involvement in a terrible car crash, in Paris. Ten minutes later further reports suggested the Paris Police had arrived at the scene, that Dodi and his Driver were dead, Diana's Bodyguard had entered into a deep coma, and the unconscious Diana had been taken to Hospital.

Throughout the night this horrific sequence of events held the watching TV public of North America in a vice like grip. Then, ineluctably the tragic news spread around the World, and we all had to conceive of the inconceivable, that our beloved Princess was no more. The wishes and aspirations of billions of people who believed in Diana's star were suddenly ruptured by grief in a split second. Our hopes and dreams for what she had represented were snuffed out, and suddenly we faced the realization that the end of an outstanding era had come to pass. Diana's tragic demise was literally scored on the hearts and souls of all who watched or heard the news, and we wept, because a heavenly star of infinite promise had fallen, exploding into a thousand of pieces!

THE STAR ASCENDS

Through tears many people sensed that Diana Spencer had ascended into heaven as a perfectly imperfect human being, becoming an Angel of vast luminosity. The Queen of everyone's heart had transcended into heaven surfing on waves of love, and whilst people wept out their adoration for her, they also impressed upon their own hearts all that she had meant to them.

Indeed, what we saw at her death was the transformation of the people of the world, from a 'literal' state of being into a 'metaphysical' reality, and in consequence a vastly new perception was born. At her passing millions of people shocked and bruised to their core wept openly, demonstrating the largest global grieving ever witnessed in modern history. The demand for news literally out-bid the stocks of paper on which the news was printed. Television viewer statistics soared into stratospheric proportions as 3.5 billion people, over half the world's population of 5.84 billion in 1997, watched the seven days leading up to the Funeral, marking that day as the saddest September 6th in recorded history!

Bizarrely there also occurred a pronounced flower shortage whilst millions of bouquets, exuding love, admiration, awe, and compassion, were laid at the tunnel where she died, before the stately gates of Kensington Palace, Buckingham Palace, the Spencer ancestral seat at Althorp House, and next to Churches and Temples across the world—all these places became ritualized shrines to her memory!

Next to Kensington Palace, where of course she had spent much of her Royal existence, Kensington Gardens burned with candles around virtually every tree, with flowers, Teddy Bears, Queen of Heart Cards, hand painted pictures, love poems, declarations, citations of peace, compassionate outpourings, photographs, and paintings. Love flags fluttered in the trees and bushes or were attached to the ornamental railings of her home. A field of blooms was laid like a vast lawn of woe before the Palace gates. Huge fan shapes of Lilies and Roses decorated the ground wherever one walked, whilst people poured out their grief at the tragedy of her death.

Diana's passing allowed an expression of people's woe for their own lack of intimacy and belonging to the Divine Female archetype. Her passing allowed an act of expiation for all lives lost, and a collective healing brewed as people held tokens in their hands that blessed her on her flight to paradise, for Diana had become an ascended Angel, as most people felt.

The personal life of Diana Princess of Wales had become an open book, the imperfect human being had become a divinely elevated icon. Even the literalists and cynics who had mocked her were powerless to stop the wave of transformation that moved each person's soul, which quaked the hearts and minds of all beings. The once torn and abused pages of Diana's short story suddenly came together in a new perspective, as we felt the true import and purpose of her life—with all its loss and gain—both her beauty and her bulimia came together in a new meaning that very few people could have guessed would have happened for them.

Like a Princess in a Fairy Tale, the imperfections of Diana took on divine proportions. Like Cinders joyously meeting her Prince and living a new life packed with a new way of loving. Yet on this occasion Diana became an Angel, and the projections we sent forth were bathed in our tears, awe, and yearning. A collective force surged around the world, as a voltage of repressed energy scattered spiritual imagery and sacred iconography everywhere.

AN ARCHETYPAL SHIFT

Perhaps you can remember other epoch-making events such as Diana's epitaph, for those days were alive in the spirit of the global collective, and now are written about in the chronicles of history. Do you remember the assassination of President John Frederick Kennedy on November 22nd 1963 in Dallas, the Memphis shooting of Dr. Martin Luther King Jr on April 4th, 1968, the killing of Robert Francis Kennedy on June 6th, 1968? Similarly, Diana's transition was an expression of deep world sorrow, mixed with regret, loss, and recrimination—for the passing of the 'anointed one' is a terrible thing to behold.

Around the time when Diana's coffin left Kensington Palace on September 6th, 1997 en route to Westminster Abbey for the Funeral, two geostationary operational satellites in orbit 22,300 miles over the equator, detected a huge shift in the globe's magnetic field that forever altered the way established science views the planet. Studies conducted by Princeton University found that the correlation between the shift in the earth's magnetic field, and the events surrounding Diana's passing were in coherence.

A similar recording was also measured when the first plane hit the World Trade Centre on September 9th, 2001. Then again fifteen minutes before the next plane hit the second tower, the operational satellites registered another electro-magnetic shift within the planet's atmosphere—but what had created this phenomenon?

My firm belief is it that the amount of heartfelt compassion aroused by human sorrow at the loss of Diana was the igniting force. Her passionate soul was the dynamo that awakened love, adoration and reverence within the hearts of the people of the world. This love was vast, and so at her Funeral a similarly gargantuan wave of emotion arose from the heart of the world, moving the planet's magnetic field.

You see, the earth's field is stimulated by the temperature of every feeling we humans experience in response to war, peace, economic scarcity, abundance, societal loss or gain, or climate change. Human emotions are at the leading edge of human evolution. The organization 'Heart-Math' has discovered this very particularly, by measuring the human heart and recognizing it to have an energy field five thousand times greater than the energy of the human brain.

Diana's death created a spontaneous flood of feeling, as the archetypal flow of force from deep within human beings burst forth. This flood came from a place possibly far beyond our personal ability to comprehend. This awakening became a conduit that centered billons of people into 'wholeness'. Like the prayers, incantations or anthems that lift our minds into the other-worldly essence of the sacred, a vast archetypal flow of force arose from our collective mourning, percolating up from that deep mysterious center for all things, the 'collective unconscious'. Then it poured into our bodies, literally startling our cells.

Consequently the citizens of the world were recalibrated into a new way of being, and lives that would never be the same again, as people were moved to an empathic wholeness, resonating a deep desire for greater inclusivity throughout life and with fellow citizens everywhere. This seismic quake opened a vast current of energy from within the field of the feminine principle. This current still releases its impulse today as a new expression of the Divine Feminine within all of us.

Diana as Hunted Goddess

*'It is a point to remember that of all the ironies about
Diana, perhaps the greatest was this—a girl given the
name of the ancient goddess of hunting, was in the end,
the most hunted person of the modern age.'*
Charles Spencer

Diana Spencer was named after the Roman Goddess of the
Hunt and the Moon. The Romans and Greeks adored the
nature of the Goddess Diana, although the Greeks knew her
as Artemis. Diana was the personification of the liberated,
independent spirit within the feminine principle—the one
who sought to define her own goals and exist in a terrain of
her own choosing—a spirit with the evolving status and
illumination of the modern woman, a woman who enables
herself to feel whole without a male partner. No masculine
approval need be requested via Father, Husband, or Lover,
for she finds her own work and interests nurturing her. Her
identity and sense of self-worth are based upon purely who
she is, rather than on the conventional status of her marriage.
As Goddess of the Hunt in pursuit of her own quarry,
Diana aimed at her targets, knowing that the silver light of
her arrows would unerringly meet their mark.

The name Diana in the Greek language is derived from
the magic of turning darkness into daylight and was closely
associated with the Moon. In Rome the Goddess Diana was
believed to assist childbirth, for it was believed that children
were born in conjunction with the lunar cycles of the Moon.

Consequently, Diana was considered to preserve mankind by the healing nature of childbirth.

The Goddess Diana was mostly accompanied by the Nymphs who were her sisters, in the form of Egeria associated with the rivers, and Virbius linked with the mountains and woodlands. Thus, Diana the Conscious Virgin placed great intimacy in her maidens, for her women were unconstrained by domesticity, and beyond the control of any male. In her role as liberationist, Diana was revered as a patroness of lower-class citizens, and thus all slaves could receive asylum in her temples.

Like the Goddess Diana, the Princess of Wales followed alongside her mythological counterpart, becoming an inspiration to women everywhere. Indeed, one Trustee of the Paradise House Association, a learning center for disabled adults visited by Diana in 1983, commented on the Princess's profound grace and simplicity.

'The Princess had something about her that lifted one up, and which had an effect on absolutely everyone. There was a glorious radiance and candid warmth about her, as well as an astonishing beauty. One could sense her vulnerability, and I noticed when she leaned over and listened intently to several of the caregivers, she gave them her full attention. And you know a year later those caregivers were still affected, still deeply moved by her genuine attentiveness. The staff felt that Diana's touch was extremely significant and that everyone had been switched on by her light.'

In an attempt to substantiate the nature of Diana's light, the Trustee spoke of the direct way that Diana had looked into her eyes, and with a gentle yet embarrassed smile said: *'Please excuse my cold hands!'* This combination of beauty, sweetness, and humanity was made all the more poetic by her grace and poise. Diana held the mystique and the magic of her Royal role with a hint of the ordinary, tinged by her unexpressed pain. Irrespective of the internal strife Diana's smile alone was like a laser that went straight to everyone's heart, for she knew what it was to suffer. Diana like her counterpart Goddess was more humanitarian than patrician, and this admirable quality made the public love her more and more, so that they would collect in their thousands just to see her pass by.

Lamentably, we also saw how Diana was hunted like her namesake throughout the sixteen years of her Royal career, which created the conviction that the circumstance of her death was arcane. However, knowing that Diana met her death through nefarious means will neither heal, substantiate or diminish her position in our lives. Whether this be true or not, mysteriously the place of her death—the Pont de l'Alma tunnel—had in Roman times been the site for the Temple of Goddess Diana.

The Roman city of Lutetia was the predecessor to modern Paris and was named after the Celtic tribes who lived in the approximate geography of this area, during the Third Century, they were known as the Parisii. However, these tribes were then overtaken by a medieval dynasty in the fifth century known as the Merovingians, and it has been suggested that these warlords were actually the Spencer Family's distant ancestors. These warlords were known for establishing territories by force, and often fought bitter battles to achieve this. It is also fabled that they form a dynasty which flows all the way back through time to the union between Mary Magdalen and Jesus, and with the creation myths associated with the Holy Grail!

ANCIENT LORE

The Merovingian Kings governed northern France for approximately three hundred years from 450-750 AD, and their religious practices were conceived around the nature of the Divine Feminine. In fact, they augustly celebrated the character and nature of Diana, and their Temple dedicated to Diana was built on the site of the early Roman Temple devoted to her. This temple site was considered to be a powerful earth sanctuary, created by a fissure in the earth, and which established a sacred portal that led directly to Heaven—a crack between heaven and earth, where the veils of our existence become blurred!

According to ancient legend the Merovingian Kings were often held in dispute over the acquisition of land rights, and to cultivate their honor code they settled their disputes by fighting duels at the very location where Diana met her untimely end. Their belief was that the vanquished Lord acquired direct ascent into Heaven at this particular soul bridge, and then the deceased would sit on the right-hand side of the Divine. In so doing the vanquished became 'God's Eyes on Earth'. Moreover, the word 'Pont' in the Latin languages means 'Bridge' and 'Alma' means 'Soul'. Therefore, the site where Diana died, which had been the location of a medieval hospice for hundreds of years, has been regarded as a rainbow bridge across the 'River of Souls'. Pont de L'Alma literally means 'the Bridge of the Souls.'

Our Diana, as a newly made Angel Star left an indelible mark on the monarchy, the Nation, and on the consciousness of all sentient beings around the world. Diana was a woman who had broken loose from an unhappy marriage, reclaimed her freedom from the patriarchy, and strode forth to create a new arena for herself, throughout which, she could resonate her beauty and grace. Thus, Diana became an emblem for the Feminist Movement, giving even further significance to her archetypal impact on our lives.

The Rise of Our Star

In truth Diana Spencer lived in a kingdom of profound contrast. From the very beginning the extremely shy, awkward nineteen-year-old girl, who feared authority, became a pretty young woman who captured our hearts and souls with her kindness, innocence, and radiance. Then, as time passed through bitter challenge and wincing depression, she claimed the right to evolve by seeking truth and well-being in an arena of demanding cynicism. This in turn gave us a different perspective for we saw the fiber of Diana's transparency, and we became aware of the very special qualities she possessed: her intuition and empathy, her heart centered love and delicacy, her beauty and compassion, her honesty and subtle persuasion, her sense of fun and tenacious search for truth—all of these qualities were like magnets for our interest and our favor.

At a time when Diana through a lack of support and a dwindling sense of personal power, experienced shocking psycho-physical challenges, she was also illuminated on the world's stage as the devoted bride, as the fairy tale Princess of the heir to the British throne. The media frenzy captured Diana's boundless radiant goodness and beauty, transforming her into one of the world's most famous women, and yet at the same time the scorn she experienced within her personal life was incongruent to her nature and essence!

THE FAIRY TALE WEDDING

'Here is the stuff of which fairy tales are made,
which tells a truth from which the world is shaped,
indicating that we are not just victims. A marriage that
has both a private face and a public duty, where so
many hopes are placed!'
ARCHBISHOP OF CANTERBURY

The Royal Wedding itself was an incredibly significant event in most people's lives, not just in Diana's. The life of the nation became powerfully affected, and the event lifted the British into a defining moment of their history. Whilst the citizens of the world, conjured a fervor that created a new form of hope and idealism by the uniqueness of her presence.

In one heart-pulsing instant alone, during the wedding ceremony at St. Paul's Cathedral on July 29th, 1981, a vast whoop of joy broke loose from the fields of thousands and thousands of spectators, which sounded rather like a medieval accolade filling the air of London, as the royal couple completed their troth vows to each other, Diana famously muddled the order of Charles's full name calling him Philip Charles Arthur George, instead of Charles Philip Arthur George. The sheer force of this eagerly expectant audience created huge impact on the ceremony, and on the Royal Family alike, forcing a dramatic transition to occur in the hearts and minds of the British.

These ripples affected not only the core institution of the monarchy, but also moved through the collective consciousness—a force that subsequently drew people into believing that they were entering a fairy tale world of a 'Once upon a Time' mythology.

THE AWAKENING OF A MISSION

'Some are born great, some achieve greatness,
and some have greatness thrust upon them.'
SHAKESPEARE—TWELFTH NIGHT

When universal mechanisms are awakened, otherworldly energies stir, and the impact of these forces became abundantly clear to Diana as she saw her destiny shaping itself before her very eyes. This occurred through the tumultuous public acclaim, common hearsay, significant commentaries provided by the media, and the mirror of her own dazzling kindness. All of which determined that her role would be something far greater than just Charles's Queen.

Through the early period of her marriage to Charles, Diana shared with friends that she felt predestined for a role her spirit chose: *'an occupation more compassionate or humanitarian in nature than anything I see at the moment!'* Somehow, she knew deep within her soul, that the future would be defined by a vocation, and not just by the role of the Princess of Wales, a role that was becoming so over-amplified by the Media.

From the very beginning, as the taciturn nineteen-year old Cinderella gained her Prince Charming and carried with her hope, faith, promise, and love—qualities that most brides yearn for—at the same time another powerful force was present, because Diana's Prince would eventually become King and she the Mother of Kings. Diana carried with her not just the joy of her own love, but also the dreams of the whole nation. Secretly, Diana had expressed to her close friends that she felt she was born for greatness, and not just as a Princess, but within a role of much greater import.

In the lives of we onlookers, the fairy tale of Diana and Charles sustained itself for some time, endorsed by Diana as the cherishing Mother of her two beautiful boys. The unconditional love she gave the boys shone forth, for Diana broke from the rigors of Royal protocol by taking her sons on State Visits to foreign lands, rather than leaving them behind in the care of strangers. As William and Harry grew, we witnessed time and time again the boundless love and fun she had with them. Do you remember the delightful image of the laughing Mother on the Roller Coaster ride with her two boys, or overseeing their swimming whilst on vacation in the Caribbean? The Media may have given us these insights, yet we also saw the vision of Diana's seemingly 'unroyal' behavior breaking the spell of the cool, removed, emotionally withdrawn Queen and her severe Prince Consort.

Diana took on the weight of the Windsor dynasty by herself, for in that kingdom she experienced little of the compassion or kindness shown to her outside the Royal Household. Diana on several occasions during these evolving times commented on the incongruent nature of her own growing beliefs, and those of the Queen.

'I'm much closer to the people at the bottom than the people at the top!' she said.

It never occurred to Diana, or anyone else for that matter, that the empathy she possessed could be as powerful a force as any intellect. Whereas today the prevalence of alternative states of consciousness such as Dyslexia, Synesthesia, Aspergers Syndrome, Autism or Down's Syndrome, have led us to reassess the developing maturity of the individual. Instead, we see academic brilliance and social appropriateness through a very different lens from thirty years ago. For there are many ways of reaching joyous success today in our complex world, and not just by focusing on the mental skills of intellectual prowess.

With respect for her exalted station, Diana felt the once loving nature of the Queen had changed, had become severe, that Her Majesty had become cocooned in the patriarchal considerations of Royalty alone. This she felt had evolved over many years, although the initial shift in personality had occurred when Elizabeth Mountbatten became Elizabeth Regina in 1953. The radiant charm of her younger days, the blithe and joyous love we witness in the Pathe-News films, or in press photos of the newly wedded Elizabeth and Philip, appeared spellbinding to the people of the world at that time, and yet rarely occurred as the Queen moved through her salad days, drenched in the august responsibility of her role.

At the same time, it would be remiss or inappropriate if we didn't recognize Her Majesty's devotion to her nation as impeccable. Elizabeth has succeeded as one of the most gracious figureheads of the State for all time, in boundless ways far beyond the focus of the United Kingdom. Yet still, when the inexperienced or callow nature of Diana became too vulnerable or insecure, this behavior irritated the Royal personage, and little support was offered to the inexperienced novitiate.

Diana's enduring spirit, her search for joy, her febrile love, and her deep desire to heal, moved her to desire greater transparency, whilst at the same time Royal protocol held her implacably to rigid social form. The 'firm' made sure that her marriage to Charles simply ticked over, and how ironic this was for Diana, when as the People's Princess she was loved by so many people around the globe—adored for her beauty, kindness, and charm, yet at home she felt so unloved. Therefore, she was pitched into deciding who or what mattered most to her?

Then there was the overt information about Prince Charles' affair with Camilla Parker Bowles. This hit Diana hard although she continued smiling and serving her state duties with charm and grace. Until such time that it is, when she could no longer be part of the deception. No way could she attempt to live out the self-esteem of a brilliant young woman and be socially compromised. No longer would she allow herself to suffer in a world that hardly knew what she endured. As her public persona radiated in wondrous ways, as she became the keen supporter of those who suffered, something needed to change within the fundamental nature of her own life!

THE ROYAL CRISIS

*'Was there ever before a woman in history, who gave up
her Queendom because she would not accept a
fraudulent relationship?'*
MARION WOODMAN

Then suddenly in 1992 the specter of change reared its head
as the Queen met a point of extreme personal crisis, for this
was the year Her Majesty experienced the ghastliest of times.
Her daughter and second son were divorced from their
respective spouses. Diana shared her 'true story' publicly,
through the infamous book written by Andrew Morton, and
in November that year the state apartments of Windsor
Castle, the home that the Queen loved so dearly, and which
represented thousands of years of monarchy, suffered a
terrible and devastating fire. That year was called the Queen's
'annus horribilis'!

It was obvious to all that something profound and mighty
needed to shift within the nature of the British monarchy,
within the firm of the Royal Household, within the
expectations and state legalities of Government, and Diana
became the liberator. Truth has a power only the courageous
can handle, and Diana as the voice of change seized this
opportunity, measuring herself in the context of *'it's okay to
live a life that others won't understand'*, Diana spoke more and
more openly about her conflicts, and refused to remain the

silent Prisoner of Wales. By so doing she changed the weight and might of history, altering its trajectory to a wholly different course.

Diana's profound need to evolve was a full-blooded, full-bodied reality, but not as an outer spectacle as was claimed by her critics. She wished to grow beyond her faltering physical presence, beyond the feeble voice delivery, beyond the shamed silence and the two suicide attempts, beyond the fundamental loneliness she felt in her marriage, beyond the crippling sense of private ridicule whilst she suffered the depression of Bulimia. Indeed, Diana's public admission in 1994 about having been held in the grip of chronic Bulimia, in a culture weaned on 'denial', was possibly one of her bravest acts, and as a result of this disclosure, she was granted a wave of permission from a multitude of people who also needed to speak about their condition. This was the power of the voice of change enlivened in action, liberated in truth, and daring in nature.

'In 1994 post Diana's revelation about her Bulimia, the London Institute of Psychiatry noted there were 60,000 fresh cases reported. Since that initial spike the number of suspected Bulimic cases has halved in the UK—a trend attributed to the so called 'Diana Effect', which persuaded so many sufferers to seek treatment.'
Tina Brown
The Diana Chronicles, June 2007

Of course, when Andrew Morton's book 'Diana: Her True Story, In Her Own Words' was first serialized in the tabloid press of 1992, a huge wave hit the royal establishment, and Diana's bid for freedom became fully public. Diana commented on this to close friends, suggesting how healed she felt by the emergence of the book, and that for the first time in years she felt she could actually sleep and then wake in peace—Diana was a notorious insomniac. Through this newfound relaxation grew confidence, and Diana found techniques to ride out the pernicious jibes and corrosive vilifications emerging from both Courtiers, Parliament, and Media alike. She literally refused to ingest the toxins that had been poisoning her. Not that she found this easy to do, yet her soul was determined and willing to bravely surmount all the Court ribaldry and Establishment disapprobation.

LIVING DANGEROUSLY

Diana's keen sensitivity and burgeoning intuition meant that she could also live impetuously, gambling with life, and moving into possible danger zones. And this wild force stood her in good stead when finally, she needed to protect her sensibility, her boys, her wealth, her happiness, and her social position. Using keen intuition Diana negotiated a divorce compromise with Buckingham Palace in 1996, engineering her desired outcome with the Queen and Prince Philip. And even though the HRH title was removed from her, the core substance of Diana Princess of Wales was intact, and of course she had access to her two adoring sons. Her new courage, new way of being, and new values brought a joy and freedom that shifted her life force exponentially making the walls of Buckingham Palace shake with uncertainty.

When Sarah Ferguson, Duchess of York commented: 'No woman leaves the Royal Family with her head!' we know Diana certainly did, albeit her title was transformed. Through the crises that enveloped her, she discerned ways of expressing her creativity to determine her destiny, just like her Goddess namesake. This she did whilst surrounded by the favor of a few immensely supportive friends. At the same time she believed in the charge of her instinct to serve those who suffered, believed in the public that supported her, believed in the otherworldly presence of Spirit, and it was these strong bonds that gave her the courage to decide what her future dreams could be.

Diana Finds Her Voice

'If words arise from the heart, they enter the heart.
If words arise from the tongue alone, they will not pass
between the ears.'
RUMI

As Diana healed from separation, she also began to own her voice, using our techniques to further develop her courage and physical presence. She purged the decaying sweetness of the Fairy Story and found psychic freedom opening a field of charisma, which we worked together, to enable her to acquire greater awareness of her vocal power. In finding this freedom she became fascinated by the notion that she had a signature note, which meant she could uniquely own her authentic voice and express exactly what she truly cared about—speaking from her heart. This in turn allowed her soul to sing, allowed her to feel stillness and gravitas, allowed her cortisol levels (the stress hormone that had plagued her during the early years) to become balanced. All the processes we used I will share with you in Chapter 2, so that you alone can find your own liberated voice, and the authenticity that arises from its use, just like Diana.

A LIFE OF DEDICATION

'But your greatest gift Diana was your intuition, and it was a gift you used wisely. This is what underpinned all your other wonderful attributes, and if we look to analyse what it was about you that had such a wide appeal, we can find it in your instinctive feel for what was really important in all our lives. Without your God-given sensitivity we would still be immersed in great ignorance concerning the anguish of Aids and HIV sufferers, the plight of the homeless, the isolation of lepers, and the random destruction of landmines.'
CHARLES SPENCER

Diana, the People's Princess, became the Queen of Everyone's Hearts and an Ambassadress for Peace, purely through the instrument of her unique love, the tenderness of her compassion, and the organizations that were enthralled by her beauty. When Diana shook the hands of AIDS patients without gloves, she shook the world into a new reality. When Diana touched the arm of someone with AIDS, the taboo about the disease was completely alleviated, and when one patient agreed to have their photograph taken with the Princess, Diana remained in loyal contact with him throughout his life. Diana fashioned her devotion and dedication from experiences like this so that she could develop her own unique way of bringing healing to her people.

Moreover, since her divorce from Charles, Diana particularly honed her unique vibration with a special mixture of grace, charm and humor. These were the qualities that eventually cultivated her outstanding radiance, a charisma that surprised many and literally melted grown men's bones—Prime Ministers, Presidents, Ministers, Celebrated Actors, CEO's, leading Socialites all wished to bask for an hour or so in her unique radiance. Accolades about her seeped into the consciousness of the collective, affecting even the most diehard cynics who had viewed Diana as silly, thick as a plank, immature, scandalous, and emotionally or psychologically imbalanced. To the contrary, Diana had a completely different sensibility, for she was something they didn't understand. This meant she felt acute sensitivity about people and all of their injustices. When she owned this knowledge, she also began to transmute her insecurities, moving into the confidence that opened her to become the most famous woman of the world, shining a force which outshone other celebrities, because her ego was tuned to charity.

TOUCHED BY A HUMAN ANGEL

Then at her death, and during the months post that terrible time, this voltage became nothing less than incandescent. For Diana's earthly personality had transcended, and thus she had become a spiritual force that revitalized the hearts and souls of people all over the planet. Folk talked about being activated or shaken by her otherworldly power, and still do. People spoke of being healed from major and minor ailments, some of which took on supernatural intensity. People who had never understood tradition or ritual, not knowing how such activities could be perceived as transformative, felt their energy shift from the physical into the subtle or spiritual body. Renewed faith in the Divine was fostered by those who experienced visions of Diana, Mother Mary, Jesus, Buddha, Krishna, and the Angels. And we began to see that Diana's death had released an archetypal impulse into the creation of a new way of being, within the feminine aspect of our creation. This force was positively seismic, with its effect rippling out, and still remains with us today.

This special force is universally known as 'Shakti'. It is a primordial energy representing a dynamic power within the

Cosmos, and in Hinduism is believed to be the creative presence of the Divine Mother. When experienced it becomes a mighty, mysterious, psycho-spiritual power that alters one's reality forever. Many who experienced this wave of Shakti were no longer in denial of how their lives had been affected by Diana. They felt their own profound shift from unloving to loving, not through sentimentality but rather by discerning where kindness, love and gentleness were missing in their lives, and how life needed to become more expressively compassionate.

In order to comprehend the intensity of Shakti we first need to acknowledge that this archetypal force lives far beyond our own personal capacity to perceive. You see the universe is orchestrated to work through certain spiritual values that also supersede the known mechanistic world-view. The Globe is not a piece of matter hurtling through space, uncaring, insouciant, and emitting random expressions as a series of biological impulses. The Planet is a living, breathing expression of love in all things.

In essence, the universe is a miraculous concept in creation, and its spiritual laws are always at work far beyond what the eye can see, or the mind can reason. The laws of the Universe function through an otherworldly energy that exists in a realm beyond mortal circumstance, lying within the deep inner folds of creation, and expresses itself through our feeling impulses, for feeling is the language of the Soul.

It is written in the Vedic scriptures that we humans may at 'special times' of our existence become instruments through which this force of Shakti flows. Certainly, on

August 31st, 1997, through to September 6th, we all witnessed this on Planet Earth, bringing with it the flow of cleansing, renunciation, atonement, redemption, and ultimate transfiguration. It is my belief, and I hope yours, that Diana helped to bring this to us, and so we were touched by the Divine Mother, and caressed by the Angels. In so doing, we were all encouraged to take our own moral inventory, sobered by the death of the dear one before us!

Touched by a Human Angel
by
Maya Angelou

We, unaccustomed to courage
exiles from delight
live coiled in shells of loneliness
until Divine love leaves its high holy temple,
and comes into sight
to liberate us into life.

Divine Love arrives,
and in its train come ecstasies,
old memories of pleasure
ancient histories of pain.
Yet if we are bold,
Divine love strikes away the chains of fear
from our souls.

We are then weaned from our timidity,
And in the flush of Divine love's light
we then dare to be brave,
And suddenly we see
that love costs all we are,
and will ever be.
Yet it is only love
which sets us to be free like Angels.

REVOLUTION TAKES PLACE

'*Stand up for who you are, respect yourself, ignite the divine spark within, and reveal all this splendor through your voice. Access your powers, choose your beliefs wisely, and work with others to bring blessings into their lives, by speaking honestly, and showing that you care for them.*'
NELSON MANDELA

When Charles Spencer gave his touching funeral panegyric on September 6th, 1997, he made a bold choice by sternly rebuking the forces that had challenged Diana, the Queen and the Media alike. The Queen is Godmother to Charles Spencer, the Spencer family one of the oldest hereditary peerages in the kingdom, and yet still he referred to Diana as having a natural nobility beyond her class, that she needed no Royal title to be the woman that she was. As his dolorous tone uttered these words, rebellious clapping broke within the crowd outside Westminster Abbey, an ovation that then swept through the crowds of people watching large screens in the Royal Parks, before sweeping back again, and straight into the Abbey. There the Royal Family sat, witnessing revolution before their very eyes, and in these moments the dynasty that had lasted for a thousand years felt a tipping point, for without the vibrant aspect of Diana fully present, this bastion of the establishment needed to move through a monumental change of embracing the love she was evoking.

As Elton John sang his lament 'Like a Candle in the Wind' sobs rang out from the otherwise reverentially silent crowd:

'Goodbye England's rose;
may you ever grow in our hearts.
You were the grace that placed itself
where lives were torn apart.
You called out to our country,
and you whispered to those in pain.
Now you belong to heaven,
and the stars spell out your name.
And it seems to me you lived your life
like a candle in the wind:
never fading with the sunset
or when the rain set in.
And your footsteps will always fall here,
among England's greenest hills;
your candle's burned out long before

your legend ever will.
Loveliness we've lost;
these empty days without your smile,
Yet this torch we'll always carry
for our nation's golden child.
And even though we try,
the truth brings us to tears;
all our words cannot express
the joy you brought us through the years.
Goodbye England's rose,
from a country lost without your soul,
who'll miss the wings of your compassion
more than you'll ever know.'

ELTON JOHN

When Elton's glorious tribute reached its climax, a deep yearning for both Diana and the guardians of the Universe once again burst forth from the grieving nation, from people all over the planet. This power created a shifting point, as the grim specter of death projected Diana into our spiritual lives. Diana may have been missing, her body in the coffin, but the beautiful Woman, the loving Mother, the compassionate Healer, the yearning Seductress, the alluring Sorceress, the heartfelt Humanitarian, the wounded Healer, and the kind comforting Witness, permeated into the ether in order for all of us to be awakened. We felt the living qualities of her passion, how it sprang open a new door, and a new quality of the Divine Feminine came forth. These projections meant that Diana who had been crowned in glory as the Queen of the People's hearts, now soared on wings of compassion into the kingdom that we call Heaven.

TOWARD A NEW PARADIGM

Whilst Diana's star had fallen to Earth, her soul transcended into Heaven, and wow what a furnace was sparked. Through the heroine's journey, the naive shy Virgin became fully conscious, summoning within all of us an understanding that the old psychic order of our own loves must be dismantled. What came in its place was the potential for infinite possibility, and a new perception about how the feminine could be more integrated into our culture. This psychic wave began to wash through the older paradigms concerning our personal relationship with the masculine. Diana's feminine force had disowned the negative masculine when she 'outed' Charles, calling for a new level of maturity and truth. This released the voice of millions of women, who felt that Diana had given them the right to speak, as we see in today's women raising the cry of #METOO.

In consequence, women were encouraged to find their identity by embracing both male and female parts of their psyche. Men were similarly affected, and through this awakening were encouraged to blend the feminine with their own male-ness. Therefore, all our relationship structures began to burgeon with change, and the 'Till death us do part' paradigm within marriage, no longer could remain a meaningful construct for the bonds of deep relationship. We needed newer values, required newer precepts, desired newer ideals. For how could we expect one person to live within the emotional bonds of marriage, through the much longer lives we are living today, with all the growth spurts and diminutions that occur, unless the relationship is completely transparent? And for those people who can't flex the muscle of this new paradigm, their marriages would possibly be sustained by the old ways of co-dependency, rather than through the new themes of mutual benefit and co-creativity, maintaining a newly reformed balance of sustainable partnership.

Through the passage of time since Diana's demise, men and women are releasing the obsolete stereotypes, and consequently the feminine archetype in all its definitions—including LGBTQ and Transsexualism—has moved through initiation after initiation. Since 2015 same sex marriage has become permissible in all fifty States of the USA. In the same year an unprecedented public referendum also took place in the Republic of Ireland, a country known for its religious denial, shame and guilt, bringing the Irish people to vote for the belief that love must come first in their personal relationships, superseding sexual orientation.

At core, the patriarchy, which had flourished through a malformation of the masculine, was being transformed on the altar of the newly sacralized feminine, was being changed by the notion of co-creativity and the value of parity. Love, compassion, inclusivity, nurturing, and peaceful co-existence are what we yearn for, are what we seek out in our intimate relationships, and if we live so we open to mindfulness. This is the legacy that Diana's spirit brought in her wake, encouraging us to formulate our own personal revolution, and so our hopes and dreams were given a new lease of life.

THE LEGACY OF FEMALE EMPOWERMENT

'When you are gone, they don't remember you by what you said, they remember you by the way you made them feel!'
ELEANOR ROOSEVELT

Feminism was pioneered at the beginning of the twentieth century by the Women's Suffrage Movement. Then in the 1980's the movement became championed by extraordinary women such as Gloria Steinem, Lynn Franks, and Anita Roddick, and now the banner is carried by Oprah Winfrey, Michelle Obama, Marianne Williamson, and Chimamanda Ngozi Adichie, amongst many others. Their inspiration evokes the current socio-political demand to create parity between men and women, to end all prejudice, inequality, and sexual harassment.

This was also Diana's life and legacy: that women would reclaim and liberate their voice, enabling them to step fully into their earthly mission and express their freedom and their heart's desire, just as Diana had done. Her memory has a voice from beyond the grave and is a call to women to live more truthfully. Her voice was the revolutionary cry for all women to live compassionately as she did. And in respect of her legacy, let us now look at some of the techniques that Diana and I explored during the last two years of her life. The vocal, physical and emotional techniques that made her feel so empowered, and which in turn expanded her energy field to accommodate the powerful radiance she transmitted in the world. Remember, this is what she wanted you to feel, so that you would be powerful, great, lustrous and free, and so this is just for you!

'Women don't need to find a new voice, what they need is to feel empowered to use their voice!'
MEGAN MARKLE

CHAPTER TWO

THE VOICE OF CHANGE

'O what is it in me that makes me tremble so at voices?
Surely whoever speaks to me in the right voice, him or her
I shall follow, as the water follows the moon, silently,
with fluid steps, anywhere around the globe.'
WALT WHITMAN

DISCOVERING A GLOBAL VOICE

THE SCOPE AND LATITUDE of Diana's creative reach, the
extent of her love for helping people, the capacity with which
she genuinely held people through her tenderness and
compassion, significantly increased during the latter years of
her short life. Much of this evolution occurred as she
discovered ways of transforming her lack of trust, arising
from perceived betrayal, into a force of acceptance. With this
in mind, relaxation in her body, and joy in her soul, Diana

found inner peace—a peace that created space and direction, a peace that gave special force to her projects, a peace which gave richer meaning and fulfilment to her purpose. Through knowing her voice Diana found the power and inner strength that brought courageous means to affect vast change.

When the force of freedom and purpose ignite within our being, we unlock the power of conviction. This power gave Diana a new crystallized energy to meet the demands of her role with magnanimity and boldness. For it was through these primary energies that Diana became unstoppable, allowing determination to focus her future, and courage to shape her way to become a 'peace envoy'. With the zest of heart-felt generosity, Diana wanted to share these processes with you, for these were the major means by which she empowered the whole of her inner nature and outer being. Through these energies she gained the presence that you so adored, and Diana lovingly wanted you to have a way to develop these skills as well!

> 'Diana is a beautiful soul, who magnifies the role of love everywhere. Her charity doesn't measure how much her love is, she simply keeps spreading love everywhere like a Sower spreads seeds. Let no one ever come to you without letting them leave happier!'
> MOTHER TERESA

By living this, by embodying this empathic wisdom, by touching so many with her genuine authenticity, Diana left a legacy of love which still fountains forth today, pulsing through the conviction of her two boys, and through all of her charities. Indeed, her legacy is vast, as the force of this Divine Feminine energy arouses, moves through homes, offices, schools, meeting rooms, temples, gymnasiums, churches and soccer pitches.

Similarly, through the rise of complimentary healing practices around the world, we see compassion, empathy, inclusivity, and kindness becoming part of the essential pathway for the healing of mindfulness. Having an open mind is the agency that urges transparency into being, and when we liberate our truth through vocal expression, we summon vast inner fields of creativity to awaken. These draw us to remember the virtues of who we truly are, and not just what we are.

'There is no index of character so sure as the voice.'
BENJAMIN DISRAELI

In this chapter I will share with you Seven Voice/Body Techniques that Diana used to center, empower and liberate her being. Reflecting on these, utilizing these powerful life skills, repeating them in devotion, dedication and discipline, will show you directly how they impacted on her, just as they will open you up, allowing you to feel that your voice is the authentic 'auditory face' of your whole being. Your voice could become a slipstream communicating your zest, your joy, and your love of life. For you see we each have an authentic sound at the core of our vocal range, which is our signature note, which is the fountain for our creative essence, and this we will explore here. Your voice could become the song of your soul!

We will look at the:

1. Architecture of your Body—how this forms each utterance you make
2. Breath of your spirit—how this awakens your tone and allows flow
3. Movement from Head control, to Heart healing
4. Discovery of your Signature Sound—for each of us has a unique sound as our 'authentic' voice
5. Transmutation of all challenges through Alchemy
6. Persona—which lies at the center of your presence
7. Empowering affirmations that will secure you, and bring you to riches

THE MAGIC OF DIANA'S VOICE

'Diana had a unique voice, she had one of those voices that one remembers long after it's left the party, the meeting, the occasion. Diana let her soul speak because her heart became so open, and so she naturally moved us to somehow follow her through the way of her caring, into an arena of empathy, into the realm of hope. She was truly remarkable, and her voice will be the voice of change for future generations, reverberating in many ways, and with so many people.'
MARA BERNI

The voice of change is what Diana found to be her heart's knowing. The voice of change was the mechanism that Diana grew and used to liberate herself from the captivity of diminishment. The voice of change that Diana evoked is now echoed in the voice of freedom we hear throughout the liberation of the women of the world. The voice of change that Diana evoked became liquid silver, made pure by transforming the bitter rebuttals and cruel ripostes—the voice of judgment, of criticism, of nay-saying, of disapprobation, of severity, of cruelty. Then, strengthened by aligning with the truth of her integrity, breathing the force of her deep desire to heal those who suffered—Diana once said: 'I can smell suffering a mile away, it beats within my heart with such force!'

Diana's voice indicated her internal strength and survival skills, which we saw expressed through the nature of her impetuous exposures—the moment she shook the bare hands of the Aids sufferer, the expose of the Martin Bashir interview, the Andrew Morton book, the move towards Divorce, the hugging of bereft women who had lost their husbands or sons via sectarian violence, the second walk through the field of Landmines. These, and more, were personal rebellions against injustice, and they eclipsed any possibility of her being considered self-righteous, for they obscured any whiff of narcissism.

Diana was determined to become an ambassadress for the disadvantaged, for the sick, and at the same time was every bit the svelte woman of power, and increasingly so post-divorce as her wings unfolded. Thus, her generosity of spirit drew a veritable gold rush of charitable deeds and events. It was through these occasions that she truly began to sparkle a newer, richer radiance. Indeed, it was suggested at that time, that if you presented a case of deprivation before Diana, those large blue eyes would instinctively fill with compassion, a hand would reach out to reassure you, and leaning forward Diana would sweetly say: 'How can I help?'

RENAISSANCE BEING

Like any renaissance being, Diana drew great power from the depth of her spirit, cultivated during the dark years of crisis, by which she had plumbed the depths of her own soul, sinking into isolation and sadness, whilst turning rank discontent and disconsolate pain into her own unique and beautiful expression of empathy and compassion. It was this level of experience that made Diana's desire to acquire greater vocal presence even more apparent, and she wished that her formal speechmaking could truly reflect the warmth of her heart, the passion of her conviction, and the richness of her earthy-ness. In turn, the experience of this resonance would give fuller vocal range to her many interests and passions.

In private, away from the intense scrutiny of the 'paps' Diana's voice was free, playful, and joyously flexible. Her voice was made free by her glorious laughter and ease of physical disposition. Diana had a wonderfully 'naughty' flirtatious sense of humor, which released waves of mirth throughout the whole of her body, proving highly infectious for anyone observing. Sometimes we would laugh just for the sake of laughing, deriving huge joy just by stretching laughter muscles. I'm sure you will know what I mean!

It's so uplifting to reflect on the courage and daring she possessed. She spoke the truth as she felt it, and as the royal family criticized her fragility, she used their ripostes to aid the search for her own unique voice, and received even more composite strength from the people who really cared about her, and for whom she also cared. Close friends noted that her vocal timbre was the call of the heart, pregnant with emotional truth, yearning for the magic of synergy, searching for authenticity in the eyes of those before her, and rich with a desire to make true connection. Diana embodied the zeitgeist of the times, and by virtue of this fact became the major voice for change during the nineties, leading the way to a liberation that is now occurring and will continue way beyond our time.

CHALLENGING THE ESTABLISHMENT

*'I do things differently, for I rule from the heart not
from the head.'*
DIANA

In the latter part of 1995, Diana faced an opportunity to do what she had always dreamed of, to liberate herself from the many confining stereotypical perceptions that were used to define her capacity. Diana was free to create her own destiny, fortified by the fact that she had negotiated her terms well, so that her two boys would be easily accessed, and this was achieved through moderately civilized mutual agreement.

Accustomed to form, as soon as the divorce was announced, the royal family also separated from Diana, which meant that life changed dramatically for her. Diana commented in her 1995 interview on Panorama: 'It was awful after my separation from Charles, for the agenda the establishment held for me, changed over-night. They saw me as a problem, a liability, a major hindrance, and I know they thought—how are we going to deal with her now? The new strength in me caused their fear, and as a result their lines of battle became clearer—there was the Charles camp, and there was the Diana camp—after all every strong woman in history has walked a similar path!'

In opposition to the voice of change is the rigid voice of 'permanency'. This sounds stultifying, grim, deathlike, and impenetrably grey. Permanency as a controlling force has rigidly held us in thought prisons for centuries. It's the controlling call of the Patriarchy with its sharp, brittle tone. It attempts to stop men and women from seeing what is truly happening, and it obscures the truth by meaningless banter, hiding behind the ridiculous veneer of respectability. In truth, permanency is an illusion, for if it were to exist, every wave of creativity would cease to be true and spontaneous and bold.

Diana knew this deep within even though she had initially found life challenging. You see Diana possessed such sensitivity as an empath, which the public saw as grace, and when she aligned her internal voice with depth of courage, she attempted to thaw the Palace of its institutionalized emotional deep-freeze. Diana's voice spoke the truth just as she felt it and so she broke out of the stereotypical mold once conceived as necessary.

During a television interview in November 1995 Diana said:

> *'I understand that change is frightening for people, especially if there's nothing to go to, it's best to stay where you are. I understand that. But I do think that there are a few things that could change, that would alleviate doubt, and release the complicated relationship between monarchy and public. I think they could walk hand in hand, as opposed to being so distant.'*

Diana then went on to say after being asked:
'But do you believe that it was out of jealousy they wanted to undermine you?'

> *'I think it was out of fear, because here was a strong woman doing her bit, and where was she getting her strength from in order to continue?'*

Diana was a living embodiment of a force of change that permeated through all works of life during her time, as people woke up to the fact that the 'blind faith' they once held for the patriarchal establishment, simply meant they were giving away their personal power to a system that no longer functioned in their favor. By its very essence this change awakened people to develop a new way of seeing, a new way of being, a new way of behaving, separating 'blind faith' from 'visionary faith'. Diana was the social phenomenon that helped to bring this about, by holding close to the verities of life—such as love, truth, goodness, kindness, inclusivity, compassion, grace, and forgiveness—and using these qualities as beacons to light the way through the darkness. Visionary faith, allows us to see the light beyond the darkness, initiates the mainstay of our spiritual existence, and so gives us a vision that is full of the belief, faith and trust that we can and will create a brave new world.

THE PHOENIX RISES

'I think the British people need someone in public life to give them affection, to make them feel important, to support them, to give them light in their dark tunnels. I see this as a possibly unique role, and yes, I've had difficulties, as everybody has witnessed over the years, but let's now use the knowledge I've gathered helping other people in distress!'
DIANA

Diana felt the urgent need to divest herself of the old stereotypes, of the old psychic energies that weighed her down, and so she made way for the new. This she did both literally and metaphorically—for example, she emptied her entire wardrobe, and auctioned gowns at Christie's in New York. Not surprisingly, the amount of money collected was a glorious triumph, proudly providing handsome funds for two of Diana's keen interests—the Royal Marsden Cancer Hospital, and the Aids Crisis Trust. Diana saw her life reflected in these clothes, remembering the occasions for which she wore them—these were the milestones of her journey—some embarrassing, some ennobling! Therefore, she felt a wonderful sense of emancipation as the gowns were sold, knowing that the money accrued would be given to great causes. The initial idea of auctioning the gowns had been dreamed up by William, who willingly abetted his dear Mother's ascendency, helping her fly like the proverbial Phoenix!

Post cleanse, the most beloved and most photographed woman of the world, wanted to find a deeper way of touching people's souls with her voice, just as she felt she could with her hands. Diana made comment about this through: 'The first time I placed my hands on the dear sick person in the Hospital, I felt an electric shock move through me into them, and the person immediately looked noticeably better!' Diana's voice needed to elicit this healing energy, which people described as the 'wonder drug', exuded, emanated, and radiated from the presence of her shining being.

THE LIFE CHANGING POWER OF THE VOICE

'Our voices tell our stories, they are the very blueprint of our psyche, and how we use our voice utterly changes our lives'
STEWART PEARCE

We have chosen to be soulful beings on Planet Earth in order to optimize our soul's creativity full of love and joy, and therefore we're constantly involved in the moving, evolving energy of the Cosmos. This implies that absolutely everything in our lives—the bodies that allow us to proclaim identity, the families or lovers that provide us with belonging, the work that gives us purpose, the towns that provide us with location, the societies that shape our knowledge, the cultures we create through language, the nations that provide us with homogeneity, the planet which gives us a home, the Universe that shines the great light of the Sun in order to illuminate our thoughts, and the Galaxy which reassuringly envelopes our spirit—all these measures are constantly changing, constantly evolving, constantly growing—this is a law of the Cosmos!

Change brings the rigid beliefs of our time to quake, the toxic prejudice of decades melts, and the stultifying attitude of mediocrity decays. Now the centuries of cruel sectarian ideology ceases. Now the imbalance of our sexual or gender inequality ends. Now the ages that brutalized color, creed, diversity and sexuality finish. For these social restraints have kept us from claiming our own voice of change as free, powerful, noble, and great to listen to!

Our voices are a physical means that celebrate the uniqueness of our individual sovereignty, they sing the content of our hearts with love and joy, and so all the corrupting influences dissolve. Instead, we find in our hearts the power of the voice of change, and our souls finally speak out loud their truth, their love, and their joy!

You see your voice is your identity in sound. It tells the world through its position, tone, resonance, energy, rhythm, music, and the words you use, what your very substance is. Yet many people contort their lives by using a masked voice, a false voice, a shielded voice, which moves them into the prison of social expectation, rather than living truly. This voice is not a voice of change. This voice is not unique, or authentic, this voice is merely rigid with circumspection or with fear.

RETURNING TO ENCHANTMENT

'Our voice is a means for revelation, if we are aware that we can harmonize ourselves through its power, we can move from negative disenchantment into knowing what is enchanting about our lives.'
STEWART PEARCE

We live in a world that has conditioned and educated us to live by and for the intellect. We live in a world that is based on hyper performance, academic achievement, information technology, data storage, competitive criticism, and a race for supremacy. We have contorted what is organic and instinctive within us, shaping our lives to fit the norm of modernity. We have been taught from an early age to believe in the mechanistic view of reality, where feelings are suppressed. We have been taught to hold back, to be reserved, to be silent, to be polite, to be respectable, to be left-brained—rather than to be joyously expressed. Being cerebral means we refrain from speaking our truth and hold back from expressing the thoughts and feelings that allow our rawness to live. We have forgotten how to speak words of joy, we have forgotten how to unpack what is on our minds or in our hearts. The end result is that we are diminished in our most glorious asset—the voice of our true self, the voice of our soul, the voice of our passion, the voice of our heart!

Through the ravages of this system our belief in the wonder of the imagination, and the beauty of feeling has been educated out of us, and so our souls have become sanitized. The wonder of existence has been inoculated out, churched out, taught out, knocked out, disdained out, bullied out, or coerced out—we have become conditioned by the illusion of doing, which inevitably means we are bound to the head alone. We have been told to stop crying, to grow up, to muscle up, to stop dreaming, to be sensible, to be responsible, to wither to our imagination. And do you know why? The people who told us were afraid of the feeling nature of our hearts and our souls. They were fearful of your luscious wildness, and your raw beauty, your ability to be free, for they themselves lived in the shame and disdain of their own disillusionment. They had allowed their own magic to wither almost to the death of their souls. Whereas, our job today is to reconnect with the wonder, with the magic, and with the enchantment!

THE VOICE OF THE FEMININE

'What I know for sure is that speaking your truth is the most powerful tool we have. And I'm especially proud and inspired by all the women who have felt strong

enough and empowered enough to speak up
and share their personal stories.'
OPRAH WINFREY
Golden Globes Speech 2018

The women of the world are now beginning to sound their voice of change, and this voice is expressed like a trumpet of liberty. For the nature of the soul's voice can only be discovered if we truly express the will to identify who we are, allowing deep seams of feeling to be expressed. When we vocalize in this fashion, we cease to hold back the power of our soul's majesty, and then a new level of becoming emerges, like a butterfly appearing from the hard shell of a chrysalis. Isn't this what was happening when we listened to Dr Christine Ford in the Senate Judiciary Hearing, or Viola Davis at the 2017 Time gala, or Oprah Winfrey at the Golden Globes speaking about the misogynistic tendencies of the male sexual predator, and the new life of all that the #METOO campaign intends.

Isn't this what happened when we heard Diana's voice find its center and speak its freedom? We heard her lone voice cry out to all women. For example, listen to a recording of the speech Diana gave for the CFDA Fashion Awards in New York during 1995, where she presented an award to Elizabeth Tillbiris 'a lady of my own country, who is also a dear friend and whose talent and courage has been an inspiration to us all.' This encouraged women to sound their one true note, so that their voices could flash brilliance into the world. A voice like this becomes a portal of revelation, bringing about a vast field of transformation, an energy field of unforeseeable possibility. A voice like this moves social science to define that it only takes 11% of the population to change mass consciousness.

MASTERING EMPATHY

'In large public occasions, I always felt that people were seeing right through me, taking parts of me into their own being. At first, this was so alarming, until I began to meet the crowds with a boldness that equally met their force, and yet at the same time slightly frightened me—until I got the hang of it that is. I feel this was what unsettled my husband, because he wanted to be in charge, and when my immediacy drew the public, he became challenged or envious, begrudging me of my joy!'
DIANA

Diana's ability to create instantaneous affinity with people was extraordinary, and on one occasion as she was greeted by thousands of sympathetic fans in Merseyside, a mature woman in the crowd reached out and touched Diana's cheek—a gesture that was both motherly and reassuring. The gentleness of this gesture touched Diana so deeply that she openly wept, supported by the women in the crowd. The media sneered at this, suggesting she was stage-managing a drama, completely missing the point that this moment of tenderness had been a deep sharing, where something hallowed was expressed, involving the heartfelt empathy of the women present.

In situations when the press maligned her, Diana became ill at ease. Foreboding it is to walk through a barrage of hundreds of hot, flashing lights—the cameras of the paparazzi—both supporting and reviling her. Indeed, on several occasions certain 'paps' had been known to bitterly swear at Diana just to elicit a reaction. Their 'name calling' was completely abhorrent to Diana for there was nothing crude about her, and so another aspect of her development with regard to her sensitive, empathic nature, was an essential part of what we needed to address.

Diana felt everything, for she was literally deluged in sensations and impressions most of the time, and very understandably felt distorted, shy, contracted, blushing or uncomfortable, particularly if tired, unwell or ill at ease. When great demands are placed upon us, when responsibilities are august, when others are non-present, unkind, or rude, the empathic person feels these energies a hundred-fold, and this can be very difficult to withstand, particularly when the world is saying: 'Don't be so ridiculous!' 'Stop being so hyper-sensitive!' 'Oh, just grow up!'

Being empathic meant that her great sensitivity touched many, yet at the same time often inhibited and blinded her. Diana needed to find ways of managing the proportion of her empathic energy in order to stay calm, commanding and conscious. This meant being present but also relaxed, using breathing techniques to calm herself, lower cortisol levels, find stillness, center her force by being earthed, and living in the moment. Gone were the days of her sensitivity diffusing intention.

In many situations Diana spoke with a light, tight-lipped, breathy voice, as a result of living in anxiety, and this kept her in a radical state of panic. Living thus diminishes our power, and so this was something we needed to change. And so together, Diana and I created a series of affirmations that she could use to feel immediate change—one was: 'Detach, Feel stillness, Observe' and another 'I am safe, I am secure, all is well, and I am absolute connection with my core vibration!' and another: 'I am powerful, I am powerful and I will use my power for the greater good!' These affirmations or maxims have powerful effects on our lives, calming and centering, rather than negating and destroying.

THE POWER OF AFFIRMATION

The power of affirmation takes us from the thousands of negative thoughts or worries, and reframes our thinking, developing positive thoughts which in turn create freedom. Affirmations open doorways of power, realigning the subconscious or unconscious mind, which when unbridled feeds our ego, and voices the feelings that lie deep within, which are either memories of old shocks, or the percolations of unresolved crises.

Affirmations bring us into the reality of each moment, rather than living in the challenge of the past, or the worry of the future. They allow us to see that 'thought creates reality', and that we may powerfully alter our destiny by choosing liberating sequences of thought, rather than those that disturb and bring internal anarchy to our life. We will concentrate on the power of affirmation more fully in a later section of this chapter, for you will see they have the power to cleanse: 'the thousand natural shocks that flesh is heir to', as Shakespeare wrote!

When sensitive like Diana, we are extremely porous, absorbing the feeling states of other people, situations, weather conditions, nature, and other animals. Feeling sensitive means we sponge up vibration from every part of our immediate surroundings, and when this is heightened as it was with Diana, we find it difficult to process the enormity of all the sensations and perceptions, into what is useful and what is not, and therefore we experience 'sensory overload'. Living thus is a challenge, until we find the measure of the force, and then we return to a sense of equilibrium and power, rather than being eclipsed.

Negativity makes us contract, rather than expand, and contraction brings fear. This means we feel intellectually inadequate, personally diminished, not enough, stupid, inept, small, and so other people appear more articulate than ourselves. During Diana's early days these feelings constantly preoccupied her, and until altering the behavior she openly talked about being *As thick as a blank!'* Diana needed to develop other linguistic skills in order to identify what she really wanted to experience, to transform the low self-esteem and denial, into power and equilibrium.

We worked for balance in strategies, through all of the vocal, through all the objectives we built together. Diana was a keen observer, and loved the process, for you see good communications training rather like the actor's craft, elicits the ability to hold a mirror up to nature, to be absolutely free and natural in all formal situations, where much is demanded of us. In contrast to the informal and interior aspects of our lives, which allow relaxation, spontaneity, and an ease of flow.

The art of discernment was an extremely important aspect of Diana's training, and we identified the sensations and feelings that had overcome her, defining feelings, images, sensations, and sounds. We determined the power that conveyed her confidence and assurance for the people that observed her, and whom she could equally observe, for Diana discovered what power stillness has.

Once we identify what we are feeling, once we name a sensation, we immediately begin to manage its force. If we relax into this awareness, our breath and body musculature become freer, and our voice reflects this—becoming naturally dynamic, rich, powerful and expansive. You see all feelings have names, and names are sound glyphs that hold the essence of the energy.

WORDS ANCHOR STATES

Words anchor our physical and emotional states of being, and therefore to discover the resonance of a word is to discover its sense and purpose in sound, for sound is a dimension of the word's meaning. This muscular and aural power leads us to remember that all of the sounds we make originally arose from primitive feelings, those states we refer to as atavistic, and so language is a constantly evolving entity. In the eighteenth-century Samuel Johnson who created the first known Dictionary, determined and recorded the pronunciation of words, and he commented on the fact that: 'Words and tongues are like governments, prone to dissolution.'

Diana was fascinated and determined to find a voice that would match the power of her physical and emotional abilities, a voice that would reflect the sincerity of her heartfelt compassion, a voice that would express the physical power of her love, a voice that would capture her audience, a voice that would amplify her allure, and power to heal, a voice that reflected her immense intuition.

Diana had an extraordinary insight and intuition about life, she could see or feel right through people. This natural ability allowed her to truly open inner discernment, listening to what her 'inner teacher' was saying, and how she felt this wisdom to be her genuine compassion. In alignment with this we distinguished the difference between the voice of the negative critic, and the voice of the positive Life Coach.

Diana could clearly see, feel, intuit, who was true and who was false; who was loving, and who was emotionally detached. The former she would warm to, synergizing with their empathy, and the latter she would be wary of, fearful of their potential control. Diana's quality of spontaneous empathic fusion with other human beings was extraordinary, and she would often echo herself: *'I'm much closer to the people at the bottom, than the people at the top!'* Yet in all of her self-scrutiny, and self-denial, it was always a challenge for Diana to see that her extraordinary empathy and beauty were powerful, and that they would become the modus, the characteristics that would lead her to her full expression and inner harmony.

THE VOICE OF A PRINCESS

'I think she had a lot in common with everybody, but also she listened. In a very, very short space of time she was like a vacuum cleaner going around, sucking up all the information, all the criticism, all the issues, all the positives and negatives from everybody, then putting her name and her platform toward the bigger issues that had never been talked about.'
PRINCE HARRY
Speaking at the Obama Foundation Summit 2017

When Diana arrived for her first consultation with me, it was apparent that the Princess wanted a complete makeover, a recalibration of her performance, and a fine-tuning. Diana wanted to find a way of being that really drew her presentations into a field of strength. In voice terms she desired a stronger more centered vocal position, a voice that was earthy and authentic, a voice that would be alive to the power of its rhythm, inflection, emphasis and pause. A voice that would therefore illustrate her gravity. Moreover, this would be a voice that would be fully open within her body, releasing her from patterns of shy, callow, restricted tension. Diana wanted to feel her presence being impactful, magnetic, spellbinding, persuasive—and in all situations, both grand and informal, creating profound change by encouraging others to open their hearts, to really live in the heart as the seat of the soul!

Informally, Diana was charming, natural, and immensely engaging—her large blue eyes, her honesty, her playfulness, her easy connectivity, she radiated a purity and beauty all at the same time, unsurpassed by any other person I've known, and I knew from the beginning that this would be a great collaboration.

FINDING PERSONAL POWER THROUGH VOICE

'The great thing about Diana was that she gave a voice to the voiceless!'
MARGARET THATCHER

Like many leading personalities with something important to say, Diana desired a style of delivery that would flow effortlessly, that would be utterly authentic to her, that would reach her audience and evoke the quality of being spell binding. Furthermore, she wanted to communicate how much she cared, engaging in her heart-center and the essence of who she truly was.

Gravitas creates magnetism in all situations, for when our voices root into our depth, into our body's earthiness, they always reflect the central power of our being. Likewise, a voice that pours from this feeling center stirs the audience, and Diana as a woman of substance, wanted to acquire this voice of power, rendering her audience with no other perception but that she was completely credible. From this position she could ooze confidence, easily unpacking the content of her heart and soul—liberating passion, profundity, love, compassion and humor—and Diana was one such passionate woman, sexy, beautiful, sensual, and empathic.

The key to this state of personal power primarily arises from relaxation, accessed through deep breath work, and lived through the meaning and essence of flow, created through the rhythm of our breath. Of course, through all the testing experiences Diana had begun to develop a calmer demeanor whilst in the center of public gaze, a force of energy that could be very penetrative. She achieved this by initially making immediate and spontaneous connection with her audience, and thus the blushing teenager grew into one of the most successful women. Diana learned that the significance of successful rapport is always established by appearing confident and alluring, accessing easy contact with the spectators by smiling, and so let us travel through the processes Diana and I used to elicit this radiant power.

1

THE ARCHITECTURE OF THE BODY

'The real secret to lifelong good health is to let your body take care of you. Naturally exercising and toning your body in each of its activities will lead you to optimized wellbeing. And so, align your spine and feel the waves of energy enhance your mood!'
DEEPAK CHOPRA

INHABITING YOUR BODY

WHEN WE ARE TRULY ALIVE IN OUR BODY, when we essentially allow ourselves to 'feel', when we touch into each sensation of our worldly experience, we are also able to identify the contrasts—separating the horror from the joy, the pain from pleasure, the negative from positive, the guilt from innocence—and so on, and so forth. We determine what feels true, alive, vital and good about life, and then wisely maneuver ourselves into feeling empowered by these feeling states. Feeling good inside produces natural abundance, wellbeing, joy, and health, which in turn lead us to self-esteem and personal efficacy. These are the qualities of peak performance!

It's well known that physical exercise, and emotionally heightened joyous states, release endorphins, such as dopamine, serotonin and oxytocin through our bodies. These hormones lighten and brighten our lives, producing 'feel-good' responses, and so any physical or emotional crisis registered as resistance, can be transformed through cardio exercise, positive thinking, and body regimes such as a healthy diet and healing massage.

The starting point for Diana was to exercise her body, primarily to achieve a balance between the effort and freeness, between the yin and yang, or if you like, the masculine and feminine, in order to allow the flow of breath and relaxation to pour through her being. In simplicity, physical exercise enhances cellular vitality, as well as strengthening core muscles, making flexible our whole constitution.

Diana loved physical exercise, had dreams in early life of being a Ballet Dancer or a Hoofer tapping her way to joy—but her height meant that she wouldn't be accepted into the world of professional Ballet. As an alternative, Diana was a keen swimmer, an avid Gym person, and sought out complimentary healing practices, such as Massage, Reiki, Colonic Irrigation, and Pilates. These she loved to engage in making her life healthier, happier and more harmonious.

Diana was sensually and sensorily awake to her body, and so totally appreciated and understood the power of touch. She once commented to a large symposium of Psychiatrists—'A hug is cheap, environmentally friendly, and needs minimal instruction!' Through all of her physical disciplines, Diana found true inner strength, substance, and stamina, so that her physicality could support any response to stress, providing her with measured balance.

Being grounded through physical exercise inevitably provides us with connectivity to the earth of our being, so that gravity and depth become keys to successful living, through which we can feel a sense of 'gravitas' and balance in our bodies. Gravity makes us appear strong and confident, because being balanced in our body gives us centered-ness through the whole of our being.

For Diana this was a great gift and she attended the Gym and swam most days—feeling through her body 'sensorium' that she could open her mind to vistas beyond the limited personal restrictions she once perceived for herself. Inevitably, this meant that the relaxation she experienced created a greater connection with those she cared about, and so expanded the energy of her presence, and the way she communicated aspects of her life and being that were most important to her.

Through all of these processes Diana began to release and heal the remnants of Bulimia, the traumatic specter of abandonment first experienced when she was six years of age. This release created the new perception of how beautiful, sensual, tall, elegant, and powerful she was. In turn this enabled her to be bold, to expand her creative interests, which proved to enhance the lustrous joy and genuine compassion she held for others. At last the positive Life Coach was winning over the negative critic!

BUILDING STRENGTH FOR A MISSION

'I try to be there for them, to hold their hands, to talk
with them, to just be there with compassion. Whatever
helps, for we all need someone, and I seem to draw a
certain strength from these encounters!'
DIANA

Living in embodiment gives us strength and positivism, and for Diana this meant greater energy in all the things she cared about. For example, every week in the United Kingdom she would spend time giving to the sick, to terminally ill hospital patients, and often spent several hours a night, three nights a week with the physically challenged—that is when her diary permitted.

When she visited Sarajevo in early 1997, she spent time with victims without an interpreter, and during these conversations she would take time to feel their pain, to listen intently to their experiences—stories such as that of a young widow whose husband whilst fishing had stepped on a landmine. The woman was in such trauma she appeared expressionless, yet Diana held her hands and hugged her, and the young woman immediately revived, feeling Diana's special love flowing through her. This was the depth of Diana's compassion, and she was fearless about drawing strength for its expression, building the courage and connectivity that sustained her through her mission.

FINDING TRUE ALIGNMENT

*'What a piece of work is a man, how noble in reason,
how infinite in faculty, in form and moving how express
and admirable, in action how like an angel, in
apprehension how like a God: the beauty of the world,
the paragon of animals.'*
HAMLET
William Shakespeare

These eloquent words determined the renaissance perspective of what it was to be 'noble' in the 16th Century. It gives poetic clarity to how we may comprehend the amazing nature of our bodies, and the energies they give us. For example, in the arena of public presentation there is a maxim which suggests: 'It's not what you say, but how you say it that draws attention!' In short, our bodies create meaningful relationships, and if we employ 'noble' or magnanimous thoughts and feelings, if we are aware of our 'form and moving', we can also be alive to the freedom of greater creativity, joyous rapport, and achievable excellence. For what better way is there, but to create life by expressing grace and admiration, like human angels!

Just like the superstructure of a great building supporting the infrastructure of life within, our spines support the fabric of our whole being. The spine holds together a symphony of movement in our bones, joints, ligaments, tendons, veins, lymph ducts, and neural pathways, all contained within the elastic suit of muscle we see as our body. When harmony occurs in this symphonic arrangement, the spine quite naturally aligns, we stand tall, aiding the level of emotional fluidity within our lives. If we feel aligned our spine communicates confidence, strengthening and developing our body-mind connections, opening us to what is most 'noble' or great about our lives, and by this, I mean we always make the highest choice.

DIANA'S PHYSICAL ALIGNMENT PROCESS

✦ Check you have enough space in which to stand comfortably, then place your feet in a parallel position, about six or eight inches apart. If you feel that placing your feet in this position moves your knees together, then open the toes slightly. However, just make sure your feet are not too wide apart or too turned out, as this will rotate your hips and push your pelvis forward creating an unnecessary curvature in your spine.

✦ Rock backwards and forwards over the heels and the toes of your feet, and then still the movement, until you reach a comfortable position, balanced through each foot between heel and toe, and through your insteps. This will feel slightly strange if you are used to standing with all your weight back on your heels. Standing with the weight back means that when we move forward, we mostly lean backwards as we walk—carrying our unresolved past (our unexpressed negative feelings) into our future.

+ Try walking around feeling how free it is to carry your weight forward. But do check that you don't look like the leaning tower of Pisa, and so use a full-length mirror to help you see your full alignment in profile

+ Check that your knees are not braced back tensing your thighs and calves, but rather stay flexible and easy. We often brace our knees back when we are anxious or fearful—gripping or clawing the floor with our toes in order to gain stability. Our knees are very powerful terminals in our bodies, for through our knees flow our yielding force (imagine someone kneeling in supplication), and so feel them to be easy and flexible

+ Check that your pelvis, the moving center of your physicality is 'tucked under' without clenching your buttocks, knees or thighs. Simply place the backs of your hands on the lower spine (the lumbar region) and caress your hands downwards over your butt, tilting your pelvis slightly to lengthen the lower spine. Many of us arch this area, which shortens the lower back and tenses the lower back muscles

+ Now feel the length of your spine lifting up from its base. Feel the lumbar area open, your middle back area lengthened, your upper spine long, right up into the full length of your neck. Finally check the position of your head, lengthening your neck vertebrae, but try not to push your chin forward

✦ Check that you are not standing round shouldered or bracing your shoulders back. If you feel the need to, as you lengthen the spine bring your hands to chest height, opening your elbows outward. This will allow you to feel open, rather than constricted through your heart center, both front and back

✦ Look at your profile in a mirror and you will see your shoulders balanced over your hips, and your hips over the center of your feet—this is classical alignment, allowing your body to vibrate at its highest frequency

✦ Take a deep breath in, feeling your rib cage widen at its base rather than lifting the breath into your body and tightening the upper chest. See the breath as light filling your physical form, filling the 'architecture' of your being, this will make you feel long and wide and strong

✦ Sound HAA right through the center of your chest, through your heart—imagine there are lips in your sternum—this will help you focus the whole of your energy into the fullness of your sound, into a position where your signature note sounds—and this we will clarify in a later part of this chapter!

2

BREATH

*'Breath is the bridge which connects life to consciousness,
uniting your body with your thoughts. Whenever your mind
becomes scattered, use your breath as the means to take
hold of your mind, and to feel your spirit.'*
THICH NHAT HANH

OUR BREATH IS OUR PRIMARY LIFE FORCE and is far more
than just a simple movement of air flowing in and out of
our bodies. Our whole life depends on its energy, rhythm
and flow—the beating of our heart, the multiple rhythms
of our biochemistry, the peristalsis of our stomach, the
shifting currency of our neural pathways, all are regulated
by our breath. Breathing is the vital energy that keeps us alive,
allows easy movement, nurtures us, allows us to sound easily,
and connects us with all other sentient life on the planet.

Breath has magic within it, for our breath or prana is the
flow of consciousness emanating from the Source—an
energy that spreads through all living things. Here we will
refer to this potency as the animating principle of the
Universe. Yet few people are truly conscious of this living
potential by taking the breath completely fore-granted. The
breath nourishes, energizes, heals, creates anew, and helps us
vocalize that which we prize as most sacred—life itself!

'Breathing in' is medically referred to as INSPIRATION, and
'breathing out' is known as EXPIRATION. The word

'inspiration' arises from the Latin root 'inspirare' which means 'to be influenced by the Divine'. Whereas, 'expiration' means 'to breathe out', or to 'terminate life'. These implications are clear—once we open ourselves to breath, we access an inspirational flow of divine nature. The ancient ones believed breath to be the sacred force of life in flow, creating the Force, Pranayama, Chi, Ki, Ruach, the Holy Wind, the Anima Mundi that gives life its purpose!

In coaching Diana, I needed to help her access a much deeper, fuller breath-support, for she breathed in a tense fashion, a remnant of the days when she had been bound by fear, shame, and guilt about her bulimia or other inhibitions. Being sensitive meant Diana would stress about wrong-doing, and often deny her power as an independent woman, until the reminder came. But I knew that once I opened Diana to the fundamental rhythm of her breath, she would feel the full position of her voice sitting in flow, opening easily, creating harmony, releasing stress. In turn this would allow her vocal presence to resonate throughout the whole of her body, not just in the head. Breath-work was the foundation of the process that would help Diana find her signature sound—which you too can also access here!

DIANA'S BREATHING EXERCISE:

Make sure that you have a quiet space that has stillness. Switch on voicemail, dim the light, burn a candle and incense—be at peace!

Sitting on a chair make sure your body is positioned with your spine aligned, and your feet touching the floor, grounding you

If you wish, bring the tip of your thumb and forefinger together, as this Mudra (sacred finger position) harmonizes powerful lines of force within your body—these lines are known as meridians

Imagine a beautiful silver-white light in your spine, and see it moving down through you to the base of spine and into the earth. Then see the upper part shining up into the heavens—this is your pranic cord

Begin by identifying the base of your ribcage, just above the upper abdomen, and imagine this expanding laterally, rather like bellows. If it helps tie something elastic around the base of your rib cage

Breathe out the oxygen in your body through your lips—PAUSE—feel the need to breathe, and then breathe in through your nostrils, allowing your rib cage to swing open all the way around, resisting the tendency to lift your ribcage, and imagine the breath as silver-white light filling the whole length of your spine, and consequently your whole interior

Then let the breath go out slowly and sustainably, all the way out

PAUSE, feel the need to breathe, and then again breathe in seeing the silver-white light moving through your body

This time, notice the breath broadening through the base of your ribcage, and how the upper abdomen distends outwards—as you do this also feel the broadening in your back ribs, known as the floating ribs

Try not to push, but simply allow your breath to widen your girth, opening your abdomen, as you feel a gentle rise in your breast, but not in the upper chest—try to avoid lifting your ribs up and tensing the upper body, as this will not help

Breath wide and deep several times, allowing the breath to find its own way in and out of your body

Feel the breath caressing your interior with silver white light, and notice the ease you feel in your being, as though this force were residing deep within you

Now, on a big breath just HUM out, don't push, just let the musculature between the ribs support the HUM gradually, releasing the ribcage as you release the breath

Do this three times and you will notice the HUM give you resonance that fills your whole body

Be aware of positioning the HUM where you feel the movement, as you breathe wide and deep, place the HUM in your heart area, in the center of your sternum, rather than just to the left

Try not to push the breath into your belly—instead just keep widening the base of your rib cage with the effortless power of your breath

Then PAUSE feeling yourself soak in stillness, caressed by the force of the Source, just basking in your soul.

This breathing exercise is quintessential and will lead you into feeling immense inner harmony and stillness.

3

MOVING FROM HEAD
TO HEART

'Only do what your heart tells you.'
DIANA

AT FIRST, WHILST YOU OPEN THE BREATH within your body you will be led to pathways of feeling, some of which maybe intense for you to experience. If anything emerges, find a way of expressing your feelings by talking to someone whom you have faith in for their ability to empathize and diagnose, whether this be a loyal friend or a trusted Counsellor. The alternative, of packing feeling states into the crevices of your inner body through fear of expression, just isn't productive. Inevitably, packing feelings away leads us to contract emotionally, to live in the head alone so that we avoid the darkness, we bypass what we're truly feeling, we store away our rage and become less than we are, appearing to live only as a 'talking head'.

Try this exercise first, to get a sense of what I mean by the TALKING HEAD:

+ Clench your jaw, and thrust your tongue root (the back of your tongue), up against the roof of the mouth at the back, against the soft palate

+ You will automatically feel your throat close, in effect

stopping anything from getting in, and then release the back of your tongue and relax

+ Try doing this several times—tense, release, tense, release—just to acquire an articulation of your tongue root

+ Clenching this muscle will stop your voice resonating through the whole of your physical being

+ As soon as you close off the throat resonator, you will close off your voice, and this is a primary reason for why we lack presence, becoming a being that has little impact in any social situations.

Interestingly Carl Jung, the great Psychoanalyst, called the throat 'a ring of fear' and described it so because the vessel of the throat is constructed by a series of sphincter muscles. All sphincter muscles have a sympathetic relationship with one another and are located in every orifice of your being. If you close one, they all close. This prevents any debris, toxicity, or negative energy from entering the body. Furthermore, the throat area is one of the most significant Chakra (energy center) in our being, the chakra of self-expression, and the home of the Thyroid Gland that secretes hormones to help balance metabolism.

DIANA'S THROAT OPENING EXERCISE

+ Again, try lifting the back of the tongue against the roof of your mouth, at the back of your mouth, where you feel the soft palate—squeeze it tightly, and then release

+ Make sure you keep the tip of your tongue against the lower teeth, and then again press up hard with the root or back of your tongue

+ Now, in this position try saying GEE, GEE, GEE, GEE, and then relax the tongue root

+ Then do the same thing again several times on GEE, GEE, GEE but with your jaw free and heavy, and the back of your tongue free and heavy, then in completion say, 'Hello my name is_____!' and notice the huge difference in your voice

+ You will feel the resonance so free

+ Now, repeat the exercise with your hand on your upper chest—the first time you do this, when the tongue root is rammed against the back of the upper mouth, you will feel little resonance in your chest

+ Now, release the jaw and tongue root, and say the line again, and you will feel resonance flowing through

THE VOICE OF CHANGE

✦ It will give your voice a feeling base, a seat of power, a rootedness, and this is what we mean by 'positioning' or 'centering' your voice

✦ Try doing this again, but now try saying: 'Tiger, Tiger, Burning Bright.........!' notice the difference

✦ You will hopefully be mesmerized by the difference, because this can be an astonishingly clear way of seeing how we close off to feeling sound, how we lock sound away in our heads

✦ For example, if you were to observe recordings of human voices, let's say over the last forty years, you will hear that we've become more and more nasal during that period of time, locking the back of the tongue against the roof of your mouth

✦ What are the qualities or values that you observe in a voice that is nasal, and resonating just in the head, and then a voice that has body and warmth?

✦ How do these observations relate to the way you perceive the quality of the people who speak thus—either way?

If for some reason these suggestions I've made above aren't fully happening for you, never fear. As you read on there are further substantive exercises that Diana used to empower herself which I offer to you now. The exercise I've just shared was a constant point of hilarity between Diana and myself. Diana was such a fun mimic, parodying life and its people, using laughter as one of the ways that she could 'let off steam' and experience liberation!

4

Fnding Your Signature Sound

'If you ask me what I came into this world to do, I will answer you: I am here to live out loud.'
Marcel Proust

Our voices are unique, for we each have a signature note or tone lying at the very core of our physical being which expresses the creation of our specialness. This is our identity in sound. It is our own note of creation, resonating in our body like the original great sound of creation in the Cosmos. Our unique note is a frequency, a primal sound of unique capacity, individual, distinctive, and completely autonomous. Just like our blood, fingerprints, iris, or DNA it is our soul made flesh. Therefore, it is at the center of our body's geometry, and arises as a fundamental pitch that creates synergy throughout the cosmology of our cells, throughout the interior topography of our organs. This sound when made celebrates the totality of who we truly are, it is an integral part of the meaning that you possess and wish to convey to the world.

The vibration of your signature note is primal, embedded into the archetypal unconscious of your being, and equally stored within your cellular memory, waiting for its promise to be fulfilled—discovering your truth, your integrity, and then sounding it out. There is a theory in Kabala (the esoteric center of Judaism), that when a new soul incarnates, the moment of this great roar of life resonates throughout the Cosmos forever.

There is much scientific evidence to suggest that we store memories not just in our brains, but also in the cells of our bodies. The eminent biologist Rupert Sheldrake enlarged our world-view thirty years ago, by indicating the way we learn and use memory as an evolving impulse within our cellular memory. He posits that:

> 'Living organisms not only inherit genes, but also create morphic fields. Genes are passed on materially from our ancestors and are able to make particular kinds of protein molecules. Whereas, morphic fields are inherited non-materially through resonance, not just from direct ancestors but also from other members of the species. The developing organism tunes into the morphic field of its species, and thus draws upon a pooled, or collective 'cellular memory'. In other words, we pass on to our children not only our genes but also the collective memories of our ancestors.'

This theory also mirrors the view of Carl Jung, who suggested that there exists a 'collective consciousness', an inherited memory that underpins the whole substance of human consciousness.

It is the resonance of the great voice that draws the listener. A voice that is full of magnetism is the magic touch that makes the voice spell binding. Once we've experienced our signature note, we feel harmony throughout our entire body, leading to an expression of personal power, of what I call 'sovereignty'. This is a sensation most associated with true security and inner peace and sounding thus provides us with a delicious feeling of equanimity, an optimal sense of self, a knowing that one is in profound 're-cognition' with self. Like coming home to the wholeness of who we are, strong, reflective, joyous, and content. This is the experiential force that I needed to evoke for Diana.

DIANA'S VOCAL USP

'Diana was an incredible woman, who simply loved people, and made time for everyone. She travelled with us on Virgin Atlantic on many occasions, and always made time to talk to our passengers and staff, being ever-ready with quick wit and warm humor. She always handwrote thank you notes, after flights or her trips to Necker Island. In fact, we have a few of her notes displayed in pride of place on Necker—right by the kettle we brew tea at many times a day. '
RICHARD BRANSON

Diana ran her enterprise of public appearances and official engagements like an immensely astute Female Executive who's USP (unique selling point) was her very own personal touch. Unlike many leading personalities who deploy their Assistants to change or renege on scheduling, Diana would always apologize herself, and therefore she was adored by many of her staff, for her professionalism and her concise approach. Diana's care of official situations, general public, or servants, exercised detail that was thoroughly heart felt, without involving any tense micro-management tactics, and this was her own special style or vibration.

We now needed to link these authentic gestures and personal touches with her vocal expression, and used the following exercises.

DIANA'S SIGNATURE NOTE EXERCISE

Preparing to find Diana's note was great fun, and here is a description of the process we used:

✦ Imagine that your entire vocal range is stretched horizontally, like the keyboard of a piano. The note in the middle of the keyboard is known as 'middle C', and defines the range of the piano, with the bass or low notes below the middle, and the treble or high notes above middle C. There are also white or black keys on the keyboard which are highly necessary for a pianist, but not for this description.

✦ The notes on a piano are grouped in octaves, and the word 'octave' arises from the Latin word meaning 'eight', referring to the eight-note piano sequence, on which the whole of Western Classical Music is based. This is otherwise known as the diatonic scale: CDEFGABC. If you were to play the treble in the higher octaves, you would hear higher pitches. Similarly, if you were to produce the high notes with your voice, the resonance would be predominantly in the upper body or head. Conversely, if you were to play the bass notes, you would need to strike the keys throughout the lower octaves and then you would feel the bass notes in the lower part of your body, around the stomach or pelvis. Now imagine you are playing with both hands astride the piano keys. If this were so you would experience a harmony of sound reflecting the range of the instrument.

✦ Relate this to your voice, convert the horizontal plane to a vertical shaft, and place it into your spine. Can you feel that the potential range of notes running all the way through your body? See your spine as the major conduit for the energy within your whole being, for it is a neural channel transmitting information to every cell, which happens in less than twenty milliseconds. In that amount of time one brain cell can react, spreading to hundreds of thousands of cells, in a time span that is ten times shorter than it takes for your eye to blink. Of course, we can see that this gives rise to the understanding that if the spine is aligned, it becomes a much healthier proposition to a spine that is unaligned. 'An aligned spine communicates confidence.' This alignment also sets off power in other people's bodies, so that they also feel themselves moving into harmony.

✦ Now imagine your voice is at the middle of your spine, around the upper solar plexus or heart area. Can you see that? Positioned there you will be sounding a 'center note', a signature sound that reflects your whole range. Try sounding a sustained HUM into the center of your forehead. Feel the sound at a point just above your eyes. Now slide the HUM down through the entire length of your Spine and notice the resonance shift in your body. Try not to push or tighten your throat, as the slide should be easy and flowing freely.

✦ Please, let this exercise be playful, as you feel the resonance tickling you, and zooming down through your interior, along the whole length of your spine. Use the image of an elevator moving down through its shaft, which is your spine: see this life force or breath as a silver-white light moving down your spine and opening it to sound. Keep practicing this until you feel easy or competent with it.

✦ Now try directing the HUM down from your forehead to the middle/lower part of your sternum. It's important that you keep the breath free and don't push. When you ride the sound from forehead to sternum, you will feel resonance filling your whole body, yet when you reach that part of your breastbone where you feel the sound in your heart, imagine there is a beam of light appearing from the center of your heart area outwards. Take another breath, and open the HUM into HAH, then you will feel your note. The sound will feel as though it arises from the core or center of you, spreading or resonating throughout your entire being.

+ Imagine it to be rather like sunlight, the light of the breath, shining through a beautiful crystal that hangs in a window. The one light of the sun is refracted through the crystal pours out as a number of lights, which we call a spectrum. This is how your voice functions. The one pitch of your signature note is excited by the intention of the breath, and then resonates through the chambers of your body—your chest, your throat and your head—which divides into other tones, creating the harmonic balance of your voice. This we call timbre.

+ With a little practice this should come easily, and you will feel your voice as your signature sound, arising from your center. Now, try to blend the HA into speech with a line like: 'Tiger, Tiger Burning Bright!' or, 'Hello my name is_____!' as we did earlier. Try to use a phrase that is an important affirmation, something that has meaning for you, but which at the same time is casual and light, so that you remove any self-consciousness and don't become portentous.

I remember attempting this with Diana, who felt self-conscious at first, because the exercise opens us to feeling shy, clumsy or sensitive. To help anchor ease in Diana's signature note we used the following exercise.........

ANCHOR YOUR SIGNATURE NOTE BY ASKING:

+ What color is the sound?
+ How does it feel?
+ Which word conveys the nature or feeling of the sound?
+ Which image immediately comes to mind that evokes the essence of its power?
+ Which part of the sound most represents your soul?
+ Find a complimentary sensing of the sound—maybe you can see it, maybe you can smell it, maybe you can feel it, maybe you hear it differently from other people. Often there are sensory crossovers!
+ Do you like its quality?
+ Are you surprised by its fullness?
+ What can you imagine achieving by using it?
+ Does this wonderful sound give you hope, expansion, delight?
+ Are you feeling you've accomplished something?
+ What would you like to achieve by using your signature sound?

Noting and remembering these answers, may help you recall and repeat your signature note more easily in the future. Words anchor states, and images conjure feelings. However, even though the above journey in finding your note is crucial, there is nothing more satisfactory than engaging in a deep meditative state of being, where relaxation and repose create serenity—physically, emotionally, mentally and spiritually. Similarly, there is nothing more special than engaging in the special meditation process below which Diana used:

DIANA'S MEDITATION FOR SOUNDING THE SONG OF HER SOUL

✦ For this unique creation, the sounding of your Heart's Note, create a sacred space of stillness— making sure you will be undisturbed, and so switch on voicemail.

✦ Soften the lights within the space, burn a candle (a symbol of the great light that lightens all consciousness), and burn incense for purity of intention and edification

✦ Ring a bell or play gentle music, which will also clear the atmosphere of any negativity, drawing in gentleness and grace

✦ Make sure your body is in a position where you can sit with your spine aligned, your hands comfortably positioned on your lap, and the tip of thumb and forefinger lightly touching on either hand

✦ Feel that there is gravity in your body, and that your feet are touching the floor if seated in a chair, with shoes removed. Or that the base of your spine is in contact with the floor if you are sitting close legged

✦ BE STILL for several moments to compose yourself and tune into the SILENCE around you. Within silence there is a space where the infinite soul is palpable

'To see a world in a grain of sand
And Heaven in a wild flower
Hold infinity in the palm of your hand
And eternity in an hour.'
WILLIAM BLAKE

✦ Imagine a laser beam of silver light flowing down your spine
✦ See the silver light moving into Mother Earth
✦ See the silver light moving up into Father Heaven
✦ Breathe out all the air in your body through your lips without pushing
✦ Wait for a moment, feel the need to breathe
✦ Then breathe in silver life force through your nostrils
✦ See the force of silver moving through your spine
✦ Breathe wide and deep with the color of this Chi
✦ Then breathe out all the energy held within
✦ Breathe like this, seven times, and then PAUSE
✦ On the next breath sound out HAW on a continuous breath through your pelvis

+ Do this, three times, feeling the resonance as the EARTH element through your pelvis. You may see a Red tone of earth color
+ On the next breath sound out HOO in your upper abdomen on a continuous breath
+ Do this, three times feeling the resonance as the WATER element through your solar plexus. You may see a Silvery tone of water color
+ On the next breath sound out HOW through your throat on a continuous breath
+ Do this, three times feeling the resonance as the AIR element through your neck or throat. You may see a Blue tone for this air color
+ On the next breath sound out HEE on a continuous breath through your head
+ Do this, three times feeling the resonance as the FIRE element through the upper part of your body. You may see a White Flamed tone of fire
+ REST and listen to a distant sound, whether this be city traffic, or bird song, listen to the sound of nature. Then feel extraordinary STILLNESS move through you
+ Take time to be here, feeling the rhythm of your breath moving deeply in your being. This represents the great flow of the Universe, the dynamic flow that is the inspiration of your life
+ Feel how your mind and body are rested, as you soak in the wonderful stillness
+ Here you will feel yourself 'standing as a mountain, yet flowing like a river'

✦ Connect with each of your senses, and thus feel truly PRESENT in this instant of NOW—you will feel the vastness of space inside and outside of you. As you soak in this feeling, in the radiance of your soul, you will feel the Anima Mundi or the universal current of Life Force moving through you. This is the morphogenetic field referred to earlier in this chapter

✦ Just soak in this feeling for as long as you can

✦ Feel sheathed or protected by your energy field, filled with the purity and presence of your soul's light, connecting with the harmony of unity consciousness

✦ You have just moved into your Heart using your Signature Note as a talisman, or sonic key, opening you to the notion of absolute truth in the secret chamber of your heart

✦ Many things take place within the Temple of the Body whilst engaging in this practice, particularly the ability to bring heart-brain coherence into being. You will feel the chemical resonance of harmony, the gathering of empathy, the clarification of concepts, and a sense of your own personal sovereignty—the great I AM PRESENCE, which we will explore further in exercise 6.

✦ All this and more will occur for you as you move into this symphony of centeredness and alignment, a frequency of being that connects with the balance of the natural world. This is a global coherence of profound importance

Becoming harmonized by finding your signature note, determining a positive metal outlook by transmuting the negatives into positives, developing a strong health regime, pausing to meditate, responding rather than reacting—all these skills move a person into becoming more integrated and therefore whole.

Finding her signature sound was for Diana a clear way to find a new level of confidence, a new way of loving, and an enjoyable way of fulfilling her work.

5

TRANSMUTING CHALLENGE

'I think the British people need someone in public life to give them affection, to make them feel important, to support them, to give them light in their dark tunnels. I see this as a unique role, and yes, I've had difficulties, as everybody has witnessed over the years, but let's now use the knowledge I've gathered to help other people in distress.'
DIANA

TRANSMUTATION IS THE KEY which enables us to release ourselves from the specter of hurt, and the copious layers of fear-based behaviors, such as denial, shame guilt, defensive resistance, or judgement. Even if these energies are used to defend ourselves from unhealed trauma, the key of transmutation will heal all if we are willing. Then we become free and truly live the essence of our being—free to create abundantly, free to contribute richly and profoundly with our whole lives, free to exchange our depth and profundity with the rest of the world. Then we perceive the measure of our capacity, albeit this is always evolving, and we begin to really know who and what we are!

The nature of any individual's progression, or the essence of a societal breakthrough always arises from a moment of truth telling. Likewise, at the deciding moment of her divorce from Charles, Diana began to comprehend and experience the appreciation, gratitude and awe of those she met everywhere. And in consequence of her intuitive abilities, she became aware of how to protect her energies from the people or events that drained her, then how to replenish her force through meditative restoration, spending time in nature, and by engaging with someone whose gifts were exquisite freedom, compelling interest, and effervescent joy. Diana began to see that much of what had been severely challenging, was also wrapped within the mission of her soul, that all her challenges had been infinite possibilities for growth into the grace of enlightenment.

MOTHER THERESA SHARES

Diana drew great comfort and direction from the teachings of Mother Theresa, whom she first visited in Calcutta, and yet truly met in Rome during 1992. Diana created a close friendship with Mother Theresa, as she felt truly seen by the Mother. Significant as their relationship was Diana wrote of a sacred moment in their first meeting, which began to crystallize her mission statement at the point of her great transformation:

'I feel I've found the direction that I've been searching for all these years. When I looked into the eyes of Mother Teresa, I found something comparable that I had seen shine in people that had surrendered their lives to the Divine, as they lay in a hospital bed in search of healing and security.'

Mother Theresa helped Diana understand how to transmute her challenges with the following guidance:

'People are sent by God either as a blessing or a lesson. Stay firm with your faith and all will be well!'

At their meeting, the revered Mother commented that: 'You couldn't do what I do and I couldn't do what you do!' Then after Diana's death in 1997 she sent a condolence message to Diana's sons saying:

'She was very concerned for the poor. She was very anxious to do something for them. That is why she was close to me.'

The two women were literally mesmerized by each other's presence, and exchanged brief notes between 1992, and their deaths in 1997—interestingly the saintly Mother died the day after Diana's Funeral!

Diana's movement towards developing a technology of empowerment, healing the 'thousand natural shocks that flesh is heir to' was considerable, and her new regime of precise thought was inspired by the many extraordinary encounters she had with outstanding human beings, and the human potential books she devoured. Diana was an avid reader and her awakening consciousness made her bold, leaning strongly on the development of her spirit and the inner life of her soul, whilst seeing the journey as 'a movement back to wholeness'.

THE ALCHEMY OF CREATIVE CHANGE

To bring about full creative change in our lives, to muster the core of what we know to be our purpose, to resolve past conflicts, we simply need to define the feeling state or conditions that we need to change, and then transmute all through love. Any challenge can arrest us if we simply do not know what it is, if we do not know what to name it, because we've become so outwardly focused with doing, doing, doing, that we've lost touch with the inner awareness of self-knowing. Taking time to drop into our signature note, to step into your soul, always allows a moment to identify who we truly are, discerning the feelings that need to be healed so that they never hurt again, and simply become like scar tissue.

To know that all conditions can be transmuted—all we need do is to locate the point of disturbance, diagnose what needs healing, use will to seek transformation, whether it be a feeling about a person, a situation, or a raw nerve, once chosen then find its opposite. You see the law of physics suggests that energy is constantly transforming itself in a perpetually unfolding creative evolution. It is only we humans who wish to hold or fix our lives in permanency, believing that if we find this state everything will be certain. This is an illusion!

We call this SECURITY and attempt to fill our lives with its force, through acquiring possessions, roles, titles, things. These satisfy our egos, maybe by providing us with status in the world, and for a short while we may feel the ego is comforted, until we realize all is not well, and dissatisfaction sets in. Chasing after more and more possessions does not solve the problem. True SE-CURITY means SELF-CURE and cannot be created by an outer thing. When our creative force is totally led by the desire for material permanency we always fail. So how can we shift? By knowing the law of transmutation.

DIANA'S TRANSMUTATION EXERCISE

Ego Attachment	*Spiritual Attitude*
Fear	Love
Superiority	Equality
Guilt	Innocence
Competition	Cooperation
Problems	Challenge
Victim	Victor
Insecurity	Self-confidence
Judgment	Discernment
Pessimism	Optimism
Control	Empowerment
Dependency	Preference
Impatience	Patience
Arrogance	Humility
Despair	Hope
Sin	Mistake
Jealousy	Inclusivity
Self-punishing	Self-fulfilling
Conditional love	Unconditional love
Alone	All one
Boredom	Enthusiasm
Illusion	Truth
Embarrassment	Freedom
Depression	Expression
Impotency	Potency

Lazy	Discipline
Cursing	Blessing
Grudging	Forgiving
Illusion	Truth
Worry	Prayer
Regret	Anticipation
Anger	Freedom
Rage	Joy
Judgment	Peace
Denial	Atonement
Resentment	Belief
Deceit	Transparency
Insincerity	Sincerity
Shame	Esteem
Hatred	Love
Evil	Celestial

Diana found that when she opened herself to the fullness of this 'alchemy', her ability to transmute easily reconnected her with the evolving nature of her personal sovereignty. And when feelings like this are aligned, our destiny reveals itself to us. This quality of experience is what our ancestors believed was the very song of their soul, and in Diana's case as she began to recalibrate her interior world, it was then important to approach her outer expression.

6

Finding Personal Presence

FINDING THE CENTER OF DIANA'S SOUND, her signature note, and resonance, meant finding Diana's 'PERSONA'. Persona is derived from the Greek and Roman languages, and describes the mouthpiece of the masks worn by Actors in order to be heard—these masks amplified the Actors voice throughout the vast amphitheaters they spoke in. You see 'persona' actually means 'through sound', and so the mouthpiece in each mask worn was called 'the persona'—the place where sound is made and revealed!

Further still, the ancient Romans believed that if an individual found their PERSONA through gravitas (gravity), veritas (truth), pietas (devotion), and integritas (integration) they would resonate from their core. Finding such harmony meant one could become a respectable, acceptable member of society, a 'persona grata', and a person of might and persuasion was known as a Patrician. The opposite was also true, for a 'persona non grata' person was associated with the servant classes—those who gave their voice to their Master or Mistress!

Today, I believe we are all attempting to realize how we can find our persona, how we can become the Master/Mistress of our own destiny, and just like Diana we are healing the demon voices of the past in order to hear the angelic voices of the present. This form of healing returns us to our unique personal sovereignty, our note, where the archetype of the King and Queen sit equitably within us. Then, as we initiate ourselves into this new level of becoming, so we live triumphantly within the temple of our body, feeling our own personal will meeting coherence with God's will.

CLAIMING THE GLOBAL STAGE WITH PRESENCE

'I think the biggest disease this world suffers from in this day and age is the disease of people feeling unloved, and I know that if I can give love for a minute, for half an hour, for a day, for a month, I'm very happy to do that!'
DIANA

Once Diana had found her signature note she also found her power and began to align with her mission to bring love to the world, through her own unique presence. Diana felt that it was the will of the Universe that directed the current of her destiny, and so the creative development of her personality, both in private and public, was by allowing the inspirational ray of compassion to govern all the challenges she had faced. In this there were two defining moments, allowing her to feel achievement from all the work she had engaged in.

Whilst receiving an Humanitarian Award at the 41st Annual United Cerebral Palsy Awards Gala at the Hilton Hotel in New York City on 11th December 1995, Diana gave a short speech which began: *'Today is a day of compassion. I have observed a never-ending stream of compassion for children who need care!'* At which point a heckler shouted: 'And where are your children?' Diana responded unwaveringly 'At school!' and then continued her speech without flinching, whereupon she was granted a five-minute standing ovation. This was a huge personal triumph for her, and one of the defining moments of her new becoming, amplifying her role as the Queen of Everybody's Heart. She triumphed in this because she felt unruffled by the heckler, whereas a few years before she would have been immensely disturbed by the roughness of such action.

Henry Kissinger presented Diana with the award and whilst sharing a few moments with her over dinner commented that she had obviously found her life's calling, her métier, and that she must flow with this, attending to the causes that she was 'for' rather than 'against'. This acclaim for her unique work brought great joy to Diana, and as she transformed any remnant of grief into victory, her voice truly became the voice of change, from which her love shimmered!

The second defining moment occurred two weeks after Diana's thirty-fifth birthday in July 1996, when her divorce from Charles was announced, and within a space of three minutes the annulment became a legal precedent by deed of court. Yet the degree absolute was issued one month later. Diana was saddened by this. Yet, when someone at Court suggested to her that this would be a tragic ending to a wonderful story. Diana retorted: *'Oh, not at all, it's the beginning of a new chapter! And one that I'm determined will be epic.'*

THE PRESENCE OF GRACE

'When God gives us the opportunity to change,
that cannot be taken away.
When God lets us see that we are wrapped within the
inner folds of creation,
that cannot be taken away.
When God grants us the power to live in the infinite light
of His abundance,
that cannot be taken away.
When God gives this agreement,
it cannot be taken away.
When God lets us create a union with infinite potential,
it cannot be taken away.
When God grants us this readiness to love,
it cannot be taken away.'
SUFI TEACHING

Another crowning moment of glory also gives account of the quality of grace that flowed through her. Whilst on a trip to Paris with two friends, one of them made a request to pray in a renowned church. Diana and her other friend agreed to wait in the car, where they sat chatting. However, the praying friend appeared to be taking a rather long time, and so Diana entered the church finding her in a deep devotional reverie, whereupon the women in the congregation saw Diana, and bombarded her with their love. Up to that point Diana had been somewhat low in spirits, but when the local women surrounded her with their love she responded as though the sun had just come out.

The women packed around her saying 'Madame, Madame, we so support you!' touching Diana with their love, regarding her as though she were a holy statue of the Virgin Mary, giving her flowers and blessings. Diana responded by holding their hands, looking into their eyes, speaking briefly in haltering French before returning to the waiting car and her Bodyguard. Flushed and deeply touched by the experience, she remained silent for the rest of the journey.

THE I AM PRESENCE PRAYER

*'She could walk into a room of people and make them all
feel as if everything was great.'*
ELTON JOHN

As Diana shed the old masks, and claimed personal presence on the global stage, she began to overtly experience the expression and recognition of her true self, and so I recommended the I AM PRESENCE PRAYER, which evokes the principle of God's essence, and gives a celestial touch to each one of us. Within this reverence we can feel that we are always in direct relationship with the Divine, because God has placed a portion of Himself or Herself within us. This portion is the vibrant mixture of unconditional love for others and the inestimable joy for the zest of life.

Loving this source energy begins with the I AM PRESENCE CODA, which celebrates the meeting point between linear time and eternity. Through this circuitry we are invited to live in the presence of the I AM, where there is no place for the ego, and so we become at one with the NOW of each holy instant!

The I AM PRESENCE CODA first appeared through the story of Moses in the Old Testament EXODUS 3, when Moses was granted by God to deliver the Israelites from their captivity in Egypt. Moses asked the Divine: 'What should I refer to you for my people here?' and God replied: 'I AM THAT I AM. Thou shalt say unto the children of Israel, the I AM hath sent me to you.'....... since that hallowed time this code has been used as a sacred key, a sonic talisman, a unique vessel for we Humans to enter into a meeting with God essence.

DIANA'S 'I AM PRESENCE' MEDITATION
EXERCISE

+ Move into the stillness of your meditation space, whether this be within an interior, or in the beauty of nature

✦ Ground your being, seeing the silver light of the Pranic Cord moving through the whole of your Spine into Mother Earth, and then subsequently up and off into the Universe

✦ Feel the stillness of the Source around you by tuning into a sound, whether this be bird's song, gentle music, or indeed the distant sound of traffic

✦ Breathe slowly but deeply for seven counts, and as you do this, please be aware of breathing widely through the base of your ribcage, then feeling how the stomach accommodates the breath whilst the diaphragm lowers—you will feel your belly wall expanding outwards, but please do not push the breath

✦ As you breath in see the silver light of Prana moving through your spine, and filling each cell with the light of the Source

✦ Then chant OM or AUM through your heart seven times to draw all your energies together into the sacred nature of your soul, the soul of the Cosmos

✦ Then say this I AM PRAYER

PLEASE BE STILL MY HEART, AND TAME MY MIND
I AM a divine instrument of the I AM
I AM the flow of the Cosmos
I AM the breath of life
I AM the unconditional love flame that shimmers for all
LIFE
I AM in supplication to the Divine Mother Earth and
Father Heaven

I AM in service to all who need the healing touch
I AM in love with all that is humble, innocent and true

Mighty I AM PRESENCE please draw from me all doubt,
fear, hatred or judgment.
Allow me to be your exquisite flame of courage, beauty,
charity, and love

I AM in this instant surrendering my heart
I AM the force of love and generosity
I AM the dazzling experience of embodiment
I AM as Human a living form of the Divine
I AM the shimmering light of the Holy Spirit
I AM the fire of Heaven
I AM the purest vessel of your Love
BE STRONG MY HEART, AND SING THE SONG
OF MY SOUL

The mind of the I AM, the mind of God, is the spiritual essence of the Universe. When we choose to totally believe in this mind, we become liberated by the grace of cosmic existence.

Our soul's cosmology has drawn us through the rite of countless initiations and innumerable incarnations. Therefore, the one who chooses to commit to the devotion of love like Diana, aligns all incongruent behavior with the higher levels of reality. The Universe is programmed to manifest through you and your life in a multiplicity of ways. The Universe seeks creativity through you. The Universe wants you to expand your material existence, not by encouraging you to acquire more possessions, but by living a life of sustainable love and joy. Until that is, your life becomes filled with the ultimate ecstasy of ever-cascading LIGHT.

7

DIANA'S EMPOWERMENT AFFIRMATIONS

DO YOU BELIEVE THE PHRASE: 'you are what you think?' If so, you will know that thought creates reality, and feeling actualizes manifestation. If you can see the truth in this, you will be thinking about what it is that brings ultimate benefit, what it is that opens the greatest good, what it is to have revelation of your own future.

AFFIRMATIONS help this along by literally rearranging the neural pathways of our brains, bringing about purification of thought, and exposing our own life trajectories to achieve creative excellence. This occurs simply as the power of affirmation restructures the dynamic chemicals of our brains, so that we truly begin to see that anything is possible.

The word affirmation comes from the Latin 'affirmare' meaning 'to strengthen, or to make firm.' Affirmations strengthen us by helping us to believe in our creative potential. They open a slipstream of energy whereby, if our belief, desire, or aspiration is great in faith, we manifest whatever it is we wish to grow, in coherence with the Cosmos. When we affirm our dreams and ambitions, literally by speaking them out-loud, we are instantly empowered with a deep sense of reassurance that our words can and will become the reality we wish to manifest.

The creation of our voice, including the art of the spoken word, allows us to rearrange negative thought patterns, and shape the future of the Universe, literally word by word we influence and inspire creation into happening. When we utter sound, we emit waves into the universe, and these sound waves move, or startle the air into becoming form. Therefore, no word is an empty word, for each word impinges on the Cosmos, bringing us the reality of what it is that is contained in the essence of that word.

Becoming at one with the eternal flow of the Universe is what Diana wanted to muster her life to be, so that she could become stronger in her faith and less violated by any hurt or criticism. Believing in and being moved by the AFFIRMATIONS of my own life, having observed countless people change their life circumstances by using affirmations, means that I have a strong conviction, that the following affirmations helped Diana immeasurably. And so I share them with you now as a gift to assist your own empowerment, and that of others you may share them with.

DIANA'S POWER AFFIRMATIONS

I am happy with my life, and I love feeling aligned with my destiny.

I am safe, I am secure, all is well, and I'm in absolute connection with my core vibration.

I am a point of power, and this point of interest in my present moment is exquisite.

I am thinking and feeling love, with joy creating my future.

I am in the magical process of inner and outer creative change.

I am releasing all hurt, fear, blame and resentment.

I choose to think positively about wonderful things happening for me in each day.

I choose to be patient, caring and diplomatic.

I choose to be grateful for my wonderful body and luscious life.

I choose to believe today is the future I created yesterday.

I choose to believe wellness is my natural state of being.

I choose to release all anger, hate or sadness from my body.

I love to meet each day with joy and play in my heart.

I love to feel safe and in-flow with the rhythm of life.

I love to be an open channel for the volume of my creativity.

I love to feel unlimited abundance and wealth in all areas of my life.

I love to feel my body taking me everywhere, easily, healthily, effortlessly.

I love myself for the wonder of my contribution to the world.

I have been given endless talents, which I'm exploring each day.

I have an ocean of compassion that washes clean any negativity.

I have all the qualities I need to be immensely successful.

I have a wonderful inner potential that will succeed.

I have thoughts that are filled with happiness, as happiness means choice.

I have courage and I stand by my convictions.

I am creating all things now to bring about my ultimate good, and prosperity.

I am at peace with all that has happened, is happening, and will happen.

I am a powerhouse, and my soul is indestructible.

I am fearless in the face of the Divine, and know I am a spiritual being of vast luminosity.

I am released from all old habits, and free myself to the wonder of creation.

I am supported by the Universe, and all my dreams manifest as reality.

Saying these affirmations with the belief or conviction that the Universe will bring them into manifestation, will establish for you an easy connective flow with all that is most abundant, most vital, and most true to the path of devotion.

CHAPTER SUMMATION

'It took me quite a long time to develop a voice, and now that I have it, I am not going to be silent.'
ANITA RODDICK

✦ Through these seven essential processes Diana honed and refined her personal essence, and her radiant power in the world. We have explored the powerful tools that align our body and breath, moving our voices from talking heads to open hearted vessels. We have found our signature note, transmuted challenges, developed personal presence, mastered thoughts, and began to live a new reality through positive affirmations.

✦ We have seen that Diana passed through many challenges to claim her truth, and once that she had found her voice, she was no longer to be silenced. But instead embodied a voice of love and compassion in all her efforts around the world. I'm sure you can relate to this in your own special way, and so now let's understand the fullness for why destiny's wheel turned so dramatically within Diana's life...

CHAPTER THREE

THE ANOINTED ONE

'From childhood Diana had the feeling she was
destined for a very special role—that she would be
somebody! No way was she about to settle down, and
lead the life of a country gentlemen's wife. Her sense of
destiny was far too strong, her spirit so vitally alive.'
MARA BERNI

DIANA WAS NEITHER POLITICIAN or whistle-blower, nor was she someone who would settle down to a life of horse management and country living. Instead, Diana embodied the spirit of the times, stirred by a purpose which she dispatched through grace, believing in a force that wasn't altogether prevalent. Diana changed the establishment of the monarchy. Diana evoked the presence of the sacred feminine in all her beauty, which mobilized thousands of women to speak their truth, open their minds, unpack their hearts, and heal their wounds. Then Diana in her last breath gave us the legacy of activating the force of the Divine Feminine within us all!

Diana's immediacy, transparency, radiancy and aptitude for care, meant she became a major social compass for the voice of change in everyone—aroused by the huge arena of public approval, awakened by the nature of her love, and alerted by the essence of her destiny, she became inextricably bound with a force of her soul that existed beyond her mortal being. Diana's exceptionality gave rise to the fact that she was chosen, an 'anointed' being appointed for a very special role. This role lay beyond the function of her social status alone, which truly became clear at the point of her death. Diana had desired to be known as the Queen of Everybody's Heart, and in her 'passing' she become something else entirely!

THE RITUAL OF ANOINTING

Since 1066 the 'ritual of anointing' for the Queens or Kings of England has taken place within the sanctity of the Coronation Ceremony, performed at the Sovereign's Church, Westminster Abbey. Indeed, the consecration of the Monarch is a profound ritual, holding at its center the most hallowed part of the ceremony, when sacred aromatic oil is placed on the hands, head and breast of the Monarch—an anointing delivered by the Archbishop of Canterbury, the most honored Cleric within the Anglican Church of England.

During the moment of 'anointing' the Sovereign becomes invested with the role and responsibility of a Priest or Priestess, charged to carry forth the faith and trust of God into the hearts and souls of the people in their earthly realm, and initiated into the responsibility of leading nobly, allowing the sacred kingdom to be at one with the Earth. This rite is both magical and literal, transforming the King or Queen from a mortal being into an otherworldly force, whilst chants soar through the air around them.

Enchantment is a property of this ritual, for to be a true Sovereign the individual firstly needs to receive the heavenly gift of the Holy Spirit, before dispatching grace and mercy throughout the earthly kingdom. Thereby each incumbent is touched by God, by acknowledging their Divine purpose, which requires a deeper and more profound connection with all that is most good, most pure, and most true. Thus, the Sovereign pledges an act of supreme service and duty to their people, to their kingdom, and to the broader community. Queen Elizabeth II is a perfect example of such grace in action, and as she moves through her ninetieth decade has dispatched her sovereignty for 66 years making her the longest serving Monarch in history and fulfilling an immensely significant role during the extraordinary times of change through which she has lived.

Likewise, Diana's accession into her role as the Queen of Everyone's Heart and then as a Humanitarian Ambassadress gave rise to the notion that she was also anointed by destiny. Diana's life moved differently to Elizabeth's, yet nonetheless was chosen by divine decree, consecrated not by oil but by providence alone, and esteemed in the people's hearts. These facts cannot be denied even though Diana had faced vilification and through forgiveness had outweighed any sadness with compassion.

THE CHOSEN ONE

'Whenever I see someone in distress, my heart fills with such an energy of love, that I almost feel overwhelmed. Surely this is a force of Divine love, and isn't this why people seem to be so affected by my presence? You know I feel it's my Guardian Angel touching my crown, and giving energy to help me, which always feels so warm and reassuring!'

DIANA

During 1995 Diana transitioned into a totally new way of being, which fully emerged after her official divorce from Prince Charles in 1996, when the HRH title was taken from her. On the outside her life appeared to be diminished, yet on the inside Diana felt more centered, more earthed, and more assured about her intrinsic role in the world than ever before.

The divorce from Charles was a vindication for her, no longer were there suspicions about infidelity, or painful episodes of isolation and obscurity. Instead the people of the world placed her in the role of the 'chosen one'—chosen as their Princess, chosen as the Queen of the people's hearts, chosen as the most photographed women in history, chosen as a spur to prick the sides of modernity, chosen as a means to flourish in the hearts of the many as they remembered her endearing love, chosen as a love beam to shine the light of compassion into all our lives, chosen even at the point of death for a role that possibly only heaven could know.

Diana's spirit was called forth by a force of kismet which was fused by her social heritage, her social advantage in marrying Prince Charles, yet also because her life was woven into a beautiful tapestry of other unseen elements. The force of destiny that flowed through her was inextricably linked with her soul, unique, gentle, radiant, immensely courageous, and will be the substance of this chapter's purpose. Our journey together has reached a point when it's time to attempt to name that certain 'je ne sais quoi' Diana possessed!

Indeed, as the chapter progresses, following The Diana Heart Path, you too will see a way of cultivating the qualities of greatness that she possessed. These qualities we will measure as your SOVEREIGNTY—resolved, strong, brave, gracious, forthright, loving, noble, passionate, magnanimous, moral, and truly blessed. Then we will explore what you can do with your sovereignty, through the guiding principles of Diana's 3 Guardian Measures and 7 Key Sacraments. These sacred vessels advantaged Diana into developing a greater connection with the energies that would support her own highly unique brand of leadership, evolving the care and charisma that sparkled wherever she went. And so, there is no earthly reason why these precepts couldn't help you to define or divine your own sacred purpose, and on completing this read, these qualities will be fit for revelation. This is what Diana wanted!

THE CHARISMA OF AN ANOINTED LEADER

'I am not a political figure, I am a humanitarian figure, always was, and always will be.'
DIANA

The term CHARISMA is originally derived from the Greek, meaning 'a favor freely given', or 'one who is gifted with charity and grace'. And, so it is generally believed that the CHARISMATIC were those people gifted with the grace of the Holy Spirit. Those who were destined to work miracles and dispense healing!

Since World War II special souls have walked the World's stage, who also possessed this otherworldly quality. Souls whose essence exuded inner serenity, and outer magnetism. Like Diana they also appeared to bestow a divine force— Winston Churchill, John Fitzgerald Kennedy, Dr Martin Luther King Jr, Robert Francis Kennedy, John Lennon, HH the Dalai Lama, Nelson Mandela, Mother Teresa, Mo Mowlem, Marianne Williamson, Michelle & Barrack Obama, Oprah Winfrey, and Jacinda Ardern of New

Zealand, to mention only a few.

These people have all appeared and some still appear to possess a stillness of bearing, a gravitas, a level of belief which surely arises from a sense of destiny in the way they assume their role. They all led or lead with an exceptional ability to attract and influence others, to affect the thoughts and feelings of whom they lead with grace and gentleness. They also hold a symbolic status in the world, sharing values based on truth, compassion, wisdom, love, inclusivity, equality and justice. They appear or have appeared to live a grace-filled intelligence that supersedes other mortals and are often known for their immensely complex natures—the ordinary balanced with the extraordinary!

Like many charismatic leaders, Diana expressed an immense desire to serve, manifesting behavior that was both effortlessly decorous and full of passionate kindness. In this capacity she organically formed herself as a neo-paradigm enlightened leader—in fact the gaze of her extraordinary blue eyes became the lens of compassion for her time, and many commentators echoed something similar of Barack Obama during his term of office. They said that when Diana disagreed, she wasn't disagreeable, when Diana spoke a moral compass moved through her, when Diana sought compromise, she held principles that could not be compromised, when Diana engaged with people she assumed the best in them not the worst, and therefore exuded a graciousness which gave rise to the idea that she was preordained as a visionary. In this role her charm was expressed as extra-sensory.

Diana's 'healing presence' aligned her story with the purity of the inspirational leaders who came before her, as with the saints or other Human Angels. In fact, the mission Diana committed herself to, had the core theme to live with love straight from the heart. In essence this reflects the wisdom of the Sages. Her pledge to her people was composed of her sheer willingness to be vulnerable, to be true, to be empathic, to be honest, to be love, particularly by reaching out to the less fortunate. Diana's way was to live her life out in the open, avoiding masks or subterfuge. Diana's manifesto was to live the theme of love unerringly even at personal cost. This became a viral commodity around the world, spreading through the ether, discharging through the psychic network of cyberspace, and this love was her manifesto!

THE VOICE OF AN ANOINTED LEADER

'When the whole world is silent, even one voice becomes powerful!'
MALALA YOUSAFZAI

Sages, Change-makers, Bards, and great Artists have appeared throughout the ages with similar charismatic tendencies, using their voices as major elevating vessels for the spirit of the Earth, and for the inspiration of the people they speak for. The voice is a sacred tool that catalyzes human suffering, and the sage or priestess that lived within Diana intrinsically knew this, wanting to liberate her voice so that she could speak to all of our hearts in a deep and significant way, to heal hardness, and turn all to the essence of compassion.

Diana's song was her loving kindness made manifest—whereas great poets tend to write eulogies, communicating the power of their intent through the written word. Like Diana they invoke, evoke, inspire, and then challenge us to tone down the volume on the endless ephemera dictated by the external world. Instead they request we observe, listen, vision, and sense the wisdom of the inner voice, the voice of the heart, as it powerfully rises up, leading us from fear to love.

Never before has a woman from the British aristocracy spoken so publicly about her pain, her love of people, her bouts of Bulimia, or her familial estrangements. And when Diana spoke, albeit tentatively she rippled with the brave voice of protest, the voice of change, a voice that beaconed love as it pulsed into space. Then as we saw in consequence of her expression, a vast force stirred within the consciousness of millions and millions of people around the Globe.

The transmission of this special voice of change grew throughout 1991-92 with the emergence of Andrew Morton's book, shocking many by its disclosures. There again this force of truth literally burst into life through the 1995 BBC Panorama interview, as though a huge dam had breached its boundary. In these moments of media exposure, as in her divorce from Prince Charles, Diana became invested with a powerful force that over-lit her personality and her destiny. In fact, this stayed with her until her final breath, as our hearts felt the wincing pain that Diana must have experienced, before she ascended like an Angel into heaven. And I believe this force still emanates from her soul, for now she is a being of immense light with one simple purpose, which is to shine forth the love of universal splendor!

Now too this archetypal force lives on through the work of her sons, through the millions of people she touched, through the billions of women who were liberated by Diana's soulful example—all open to the spirit that stays fresh within our hearts, whilst we remember her love, her kindness, her honesty, her wisdom, her beauty and her caring. Diana bestowed upon us a legacy of compassion and empathy that was and is of unprecedented proportion.

In fact, we can still hear Diana's voice reaching out through the resonance of the soulful work of Oprah Winfrey, who urges us to find the highest vision of ourselves. Or, through Marianne Williamson's politics of love. Or via the social anthropologist Brene Brown, whose TED TALK about 'the power of vulnerability' has been watched by over ten million viewers to date, which led to her NETFLIX film.

A NEW PARADIGM OF LEADERSHIP

'What concerns me most of all about the monarchy or the establishment, is that they have become indifferent, and I think this is a problem. I believe this should be

sorted out. I want the key members to have an
understanding of people's emotions, people's
insecurities, people's distress, people's hopes and
dreams. I would like a monarchy that has more contact
with the people, and I don't mean riding around on
bicycles and things like that, but just having an in-
depth understanding, therefore reviewing the nation
and its people with greater compassion.'

DIANA

Diana dispatched her compassion through the measure of her unconditional love, a force that many of our current Leaders lack today. She conveyed this passion through her mesmeric grace and charmed charisma, living her power through her spellbinding performance, and yet one that was without vainglory. Diana's allure, charm, and playfulness kept any pretension of vanity at bay. *'I really love to laugh at the pompous or over serious, so let's all lighten up a bit and have a good giggle!'* she would say, as she collapsed into a chair roaring her head off with laughter. Hers was a uniquely special force, giving rise to the notion that she was preordained as a visionary, as an ambassadress for human concern, as a woman of the people, for the people, by the people.

Diana's role discarded the veils, the cloaks, the masks that shrouded contemporary authority, and requested that we create direct, compassionate connection with each other, for she believed that we are all one. It was this 'personal touch' that forged Diana's 'je ne sais quoi' and which her sons still carry in their hearts, dispatching her power through their caring solace, through their ardent campaigns for greater awareness around mental health, the alleviation of HIV suffering, the relief of the homeless, and the other charities they attend to in Diana's name.

Throughout her destiny, Diana dispatched her beauty and kindness through authenticity and grace. When Diana spoke in public, she outraged oppression, for although her voice may have been gentle, within it lay audacity. When commenting on the harshness and ostracism of the family into which she had married, her voice was a cry for transformation through the song of kindness. When Diana lavished praise on the children, she sang lullabies to their merit. When Diana became fully charged by the voice of change, she echo-located her way forward, perceiving her role in the world not as the Queen of the United Kingdom, but as the Queen of an altogether different realm, the kingdom of the heart. Thus, she morphed from the patrician role bequeathed her, into the more acceptable role of the peace envoy.

Her force whilst alive was like a battery, galvanized by the immense support she received from the thought projections of millions of peoples, the love of the people who supported her, and as these vibrations matured so Diana expanded her role. Even though her critics thought her softly articulated admissions were formed only through the rhetoric of paranoia, little did they really know that they had sadly and irrevocably missed the point!

Diana's most important belief was to uphold humanity's

secret moral code—'*do as you would be done by*'—and it was this resonance that compelled us to believe in her, for her very nature was inclusive. We believed her because in gentleness she spoke without judgment. We believed her as the pain of disassociation met her even though we observed from afar. We believed her because in adversity she was always compassionate. We believed her when her head tossed sideways as she mentioned how her critics had made her out to be mad. We believed her when she spoke of the criticism received from the British Government concerning her support of anti-landmine issues. We believed her even as we saw her sad and wearied face, emphasizing what perception she truly carried concerning her doomed marriage!

A HEROINE'S JOURNEY

'The truth is that in the midst of tragedy nothing matters more than our stories. Our complex, nuanced stories are the path to healing and change. They are the truth, and there's no better foundation for change than the truth.'
BRENE BROWN

Diana acquired her power whilst living the truth of the heroine's journey, and it was through this odyssey that her vast vulnerability truly surfaced to be kindling for other people. It was by living truth that Diana shaped the alchemy of the wounds and heartbreaks, which eventually catalyzed her into the growth and emergence of a new way of being. Even if her initiation as an anointed one was tough, through this quest she also became vital, rich and humble, in the sense of being the successful woman she had dreamed of becoming.

Her journey was similar to the struggle of many women who have faced institutionalized sexism, harassment, abuse, violence, rape or, horror upon horrors, femicide. Like her sisters in travail Diana was challenged to find the courage to transcend, to seek out the knowledge that would heal the ills and transform the horror into a flight towards victory. This was so in communion with other great modern leaders who had also been assassinated, most of whom were gentle men—Gandhi, Dr. Martin Luther King Jr, John Fitzgerald Kennedy, Robert Kennedy, Malcom X, and John Lennon. Similarly, Diana faced immense resistance concerning the love that she offered, that she still offers, for her wisdom, beauty and kindness continue to touch and impact our lives, and the legacy of her love can be held as an exemplar for our own maturing.

'First they ignore you. Then they laugh at you. Then they attack you. Then you win!'
GANDHI

Many saw Diana's search for truth through the force of her tears, the love for her children, her easy social nature, her endearing laugh, and her eagerness to gift the touch of familiarity. People believed Diana when she told us how the establishment had misperceived her and in so doing her voice of change became that of a mutineer, protesting against all that was treacherous, unloving, unjust, and lacking in transparency. We loved her bid for freedom, because in her past were women like her, but who had been silenced by the betrayal of their husbands or fathers. We believed her because women from history had like herself been sentenced to the Tower of London, or Newgate Prison. We believed her because women like her had been locked away, to only perish in the Bedlams, Asylums or Psychiatric Hospitals. We believed her because women before her have been silenced by violence, solitary confinement, rape, or by suffering incarceration in darkened rooms, for they too had also been humbled as victims of circumstance.

> 'Once, someone gave me a beautiful casket, and inside it I found great darkness. It took me a number of years to recognize that this was a great gift, because in my dismay it moved me to LOVE. My bulimia gave me a similar experience of feeling empty, like a void. This then turned into a love that meant I could hug the little ones who came, and smile at the grown-ups who needed compassion!'
> DIANA

ALCHEMIZING DARKNESS INTO THE TREASURE OF LIGHT

Diana's description of her Bulimia through her own admission was an act of survival, and a way of creating a boundary between herself and the fact that she was constantly pillaged by disdaining opinion. All of Diana's tears, outrage, bulimia, and other acts of defiance—even when falling down a flight of stairs—were censured by aloofness, and disdain, simply because they didn't understand, and were fearful.

What the establishment didn't see was that Diana's dramas were acts of protest. Each one was a movement back to self-reliance, because how could her empathic nature hurt anyone, other than herself? Bizarre as it may sound to a hardened heart, whatever pain she suffered became the dulling mechanism for the sore that lurked within, as she watched her love for Charles become contempt. Then, ironically Charles's deception became Diana's destiny, even though she had made a protest of both outrage and sympathy, she was awarded isolation as the only medicine.

Of course, powerful relationship conflicts are never one sided, and Charles must have been worn out by the persistent passion expressed by his late wife. Diana's private survival strategy in the midst of this ocean of hurt became contempt within the establishment, rather than eliciting the care she had yearned for. The establishment saw the action of her storytelling as an attack of sabotage on the Queen. For if you can find the courage to tell your story, it is one of the most dangerous, risky processes that you can engage in. Diana did this with great impetuosity and courage. And finally, she saw her Bulimia as a friend, whilst being ignored by the man she loved. She learned to see this as her best strategy, and she plummeted the depths of her despair, discovering her voice lying deep within the darkness. She saw Bulimia as a means to release the toxicity of the past. She saw her new voice as the voice of zeal, and found the courage to influence similarly affected women or men. This is the blood flow of the Voice of Change!

BEHIND THE SCENES

The general public held Diana in admiration, for her leadership force was seismic with kindness and affability, even though initially she hid her pain. Yet behind the scenes, the private Diana hid nothing. When Diana's behavior became overly familiar, boundaries could easily become blurred and roles made unclear, particularly with regard to her personal protection officers. Those magnetized by Diana's highly personable radiance became keepers of her personal confidences, buffers between the official life she lived, and in private shoulders on which her tears were spent. From reading the varying accounts of her life, it is clear that her personal staff were fully aware of her quixotic mood changes, and some felt they couldn't contain the extent of her reach. As a result, there were a number of staff turnovers, whilst she endeavored to find people who were in vibrational match with her own evolving capacity and interests.

I personally never found Diana to be troublesome, and I witnessed her through private heights of joy, and torrid depths of depression. I felt in complete coherence with what she desired to accomplish in the world, like some of the other people close to her, who served her for a number of years. Being enthralled by Diana was easy, yet we all needed to simply keep reminding ourselves of the fact that she was a cipher by which a powerful force could be read, and the privilege of spending time with her, casually or formally, was pure privilege and not friendship. We simply had to be ready to 'hold' her through the cascading incandescence of her emotional pain, via the heights of passion, and through the mental anguish mixed with intuitive perspicacity. We encouraged her to muscle up in the dream of what she wanted to become, and to live constantly in pursuit of that dream. For this is who she was, even though in much of her 'public exposure' she also struggled to be within a system that wanted to control her!

THE ASTROLOGY OF A QUEEN OF HEARTS

Another close aide to Diana was the world-renowned Astrologer Debbie Frank. Debbie is also a close friend, and

I'm immensely grateful that she has written the following Astrological review of Diana's extraordinary personality. Debbie has been as confidential about Diana as I have, and although we knew of one another, Diana was always respectful of never mixing her intimate associates—a very particular trait of someone with their Sun in Cancer!

'Being born under the Sun sign of Cancer placed Diana in the realm of the Divine Mother. Cancerians need to nurture and be nurtured, and the huge void created in Diana's heart, by the departure of her own Mother when she was only six, left a huge gash which she spent her whole life trying to heal.

In soul terms, Diana's abandoning Mother and negligent Husband, created a powerful catalyst within her, projecting into the world the qualities of the Divine Mother. Therefore, Diana's intimacy with her two adoring sons, her easy associations with the many people she cared for, her fluid way of humanizing pomp and circumstance, created a precious and powerful healing within her being. This moved her further to create intimate relationships, and so she created a 'hug heaven', which she hadn't experienced during her own childhood, except perhaps in the adoring relationship with her younger brother and pets.

Cancer, of all the signs in the Zodiac has an immensely protective nature, and Diana deeply desired to hold her dear ones close, to hold her children safe in the sanctuary of her love, protecting them from the demanding nature of their Royal roles, and from the wounding energies of the world. Diana's rich empathy, enfolding kindness, and heartfelt love were all organic attributes of her Sun in Cancer—a sign that promotes a laser like intelligence for perceiving the minute non-verbal cues expressed by others, which show their weakness, their needs, their vulnerabilities, and their desires—Diana had this skill aplenty!

Diana's astrological chart also possessed other outstanding features that gave rise to the nature of the many contradictions that often surfaced in her. Diana's Moon was in Aquarius, and this meant that she resonated with the broader nature of humanity, which could easily help her to project her care into large groups of people, including nations, and whole cultures. At the same time, she often felt challenged by those who broke loyalty, and who appeared brittle in relation to her rich empathy.

The empathy lodged within the status of the Moon in Aquarius, brings an individual's caring to the fore, and in Diana's case, this was expressed in relation to the dispossessed, the homeless, HIV sufferers, the dying, the disabled, the mentally ill, and the disenfranchised. Alleviation of their suffering became Diana's principle mission, and her natural heart-borne charity created a bravery that cut through royal protocol and established her own way of loving—loving those she felt needed it most. Within this she was fearless, and would take refuge in her charitable *activities, until they were draining, and then would fairly and graciously move to another. Like most empaths Diana learned to know how to flow with the energies of her love, and if thwarted, she would move to where the greatest energetic charge would be, to levitate herself once more into joy. Learning to say 'No!' was a difficult but a well-earned lesson for her.*

The contrast between her sun in Cancer and moon in Aquarius was also highly apparent in Diana's core nature. This combination of forces brought about a subtle percolation of her energies, which created a point in focus that became rather like an off/on switch between the personal and impersonal, the attached and detached, the formal and the informal. These qualities alone indicated how flexible Diana was, with a scope of immense versatility in her nature.

Diana also had Sagittarius as a rising sign, which meant that she made light of the pompous, raised a smile for those who were in awe or vulnerable, created play, fun, and adventure wherever she went, and shimmered with a freedom which lifted any atmosphere. Her global appeal, and affinity with the differing cultures of the world, meant that she effortlessly transcended any social boundary, making her unstoppable. Look at her love of the arts and fashion, for example!

Sagittarius is the sign of the person who is in the constant movement of development, and Diana often talked to me about how much she wanted to grow, succeed, or needed to learn. All of these skills brought her to strengthen and richen her life. In association with this, she also possessed a philosophic, spiritual intelligence that moved her inexorably to find answers, superseding any limitation or difficulty, which ultimately helped her to become the embodiment of grace and charm.

Diana's intense personal life was astro-threaded throughout her chart. Her Moon, for example, in combustion with Venus, Uranus and Mars, created an immensely volatile combination, that provided little emotional containment, and constantly challenged her to acquire something new, to explore, to change the status quo. The thousand shocks and knocks she sustained through her marriage were a product of this combustible union. Yet, the force that moved her into feeling downtrodden, the force that earlier had kept old wounds open, eventually made Diana brave, and so she sought out aid and healing, rather than suffering in silence. The ripple effect of these colliding energies became the force with which she faced the Royal Family, and so eventually she became the essence of the voice of change within that establishment, both literally and metaphorically.

Diana produced seismic shifts in her contact with the Royals, their protocol, their way of relating, and their behavior—even to the point of changing the traditional silence of Royal Mourning post her death. Diana, single handedly forced the Royal family to accept, adapt and modernize their modus operandi—in this Diana was an immensely brave pioneer.

Diana's Mars and Pluto energies were also placed so close together that they produced a passionate and powerful combination. Therefore, Diana was well aware of how she needed to retain, regain, and register her personal power, heal emotional-instability and heart-gashes of earlier years, and transform or transcend, through levitating over the staggeringly cruel forces that sought to destroy her, within the Royal Households and Political Regimes.

Diana's desire to eliminate landmines was a literal reflection of this. Her wish to stop the hidden abuse of power (for she knew all about the buried missiles in life that could erupt unexpectedly) was vast, and one of her biggest achievements and most pronounced legacies was the ratification of her wish to change the use of landmines.'

DEBBIE FRANK

THE SEVEN SACRAMENTS OF DIANA'S TRANSFORMATION

'Being alone isn't always easy, but it gives me time to wonder, to search for inner truth, to be curious about visiting the sacred spaces in my soul. For this is where the beauty of love lives, and this is my most treasured jewel!'

DIANA

At the beginning of 1996, Diana stood in the portal of another shift of countenance, and this arose from her intuition, as she easily embraced the spiritual aspect of her existence. This meant that she carried the central belief that all life is inter-related, that all sentient beings are in living regard of one another, and that this interconnectivity must be revered as sacred. With this in mind I introduced Diana to a series of sacred sacraments, which she used to create both a disciplined spiritual practice, and energetic boundaries, for the greater creation of that that most mattered to her—the expression of love, compassion, empathy, and charity.

Boundaries are an important way of creating direct energy definitions when we consider everything that flows. Boundaries do not separate us from one another, rather they richen our contact, by helping us to create detachment, stillness, and the ability to observe, therefore we truly remain in the sanctity of the moment. This knowledge allows us to interpret what we do best when we are in touch with our soul. Boundaries help us discern whether we can accept certain behaviors in ourselves, and others. Boundaries aid us to define more consciously how to interact with the whole substance of life, how to protect our energies from being overwhelmed, and how to revere other life forms, whatever consciousness is deciding to be. In the case of most of Diana's interactions, it was important for her to identify how to manage her sensitivity, and her profound calling.

Here is the list that helped Diana define her personal boundaries, and hopefully these may help you too…

DIANA'S PERSONAL BOUNDARIES

1. KNOW YOUR LIMITS—what makes you comfortable and what makes you uncomfortable. You are the one that decides who or what you can let into your being

2. BE AWARE OF YOUR FEELINGS—set a positive intention for today, for this week, for this month, for this year, and feel what would it be like to create the highest vision of yourself. What would it be like to move beyond your comfort zone? What would be like to achieve the glory of successful creation? Learn to feel the proportion of the energy in relation to your creative expression

3. BE DIRECT AND HONEST—this means never denying your own personal dialogue, never compromising your virtue, particularly when you are plummeted into situations that demand you really show up. A great definition of a boundary is to recognize that whatever you are engaged in may not be your vibrational match, and so walk away, whilst at the same time respecting that it may be an accurate match for those who are engaged

4. GIVE YOURSELF PERMISSION—granting yourself permission is a sign of self-respect, self-love, and self-empowerment

5. WHAT IS THE SCOPE OF YOUR AWARENESS—are you limiting yourself from exploring the wonder of life, by simply determining that you aren't feeling comfortable? Or are you expanding your creative potential to the betterment of you?

6. CONSIDER YOUR PAST AND FUTURE—honor your feelings and see clearly that what was once appropriate maybe not be so in the future. This means you are creatively alive, and expanding 'you' into the highest or greatest vision of you

7. TREAT SELF-CARE AS A PRIORITY—put yourself first by honoring and organizing the capacity of your feelings, and of your physical output. Being thus means that you will harbor a positive regard for your peace of mind, wellbeing, and ability to form harmonious perspectives about any given situation. Even in those challenging moments when the odds appear stacked against you, whatever you are engaged in you will feel balance

8. CREATE SUPPORT—measure with your truth who you can ask for help, being prepared to yield and surrender to new ideas or ways of being. provide yourself with the material support that allows you to function at your optimized capacity, making sure you live with trust for your team. ground at least once a day!

9. BE SOVEREIGN—this means being assertive yet pliable. Define your personal power which means possessing the ability to step forward in your sovereignty, by knowing yourself and eliciting personal purpose. Try not to deny the possibility of accomplishment

10. BEGIN GENTLY—often when we are learning new skills, developing new relationships, or expanding ourselves in new projects, we force the situation, and try too hard, overbalancing our energy output. Instead start gradually, gently, humbly, respecting and honoring all aspects of life

11. CREATE A RECOVERY PROCESS—within all of the doing, make sure you also have time to 'be', whether this be through Meditation, engaging with Mother Nature, or pursuing a physical activity that replenishes your energy—physically, emotionally, mentally and spiritual. This will help you to foster the creation of those positive endorphins that will simply uplift you

12. CREATE A SACRED SPACE—be open to spirit, recognize that you are living inter-connectedly with the whole of nature. Think on the essence of the force that created you, humble yourself to the awesomeness of creation, truly recognize that we function best when in the betterment of creation, when we honor the fact that all sentient beings are inclusively one. Trusting, believing and having faith in a higher Divine or Moral order, means we are truly

honoring the richness of our holistic nature, our divine selves, which brings us to a level of force that allows easier participation in the richness and sacrament of life. The Universe always has our back!

THE SACRAMENTS

Sacraments are sacred moments of ritual activity whereby we are reminded of who we truly are, what our essence is, and what our soul wishes. They are made buoyant by the purest moral code that we have—*'do as you would be done by'*. Sacraments help us ascertain what vast spiritual potential we possess, and how our physical reality is not the complete story. Indeed, when we wake to the mega potential of our spiritual nature, of the huge legacy that is contained within our souls, and how we need to embody our lives, life opens exponentially in the most amazing fashion—for in truth we are mighty spiritual beings engaged in the dimensional limits of a human experience.

Remembering who we truly are, rather than being diminished, means we begin to express our true creative potential in the world. And when we begin this trajectory, we start to live the highest vision of ourselves, developing our core relationships in charitable regard of other sentient beings, and through what we wish to create for the betterment of all life.

When we arrive in this world, we come with an inherent spiritual tool kit. We are born with a sense of love and joy, we are born with a primal awareness of right and wrong. We are born with the innate knowledge of what is fair or unfair, of what is just and unjust. We are born with an essential feeling about decency and kindness. We are born with a primary recognition of personal boundaries, and the possession of a strong moral compass—yet then life interferes by being divisive!

We find that the spiritual qualities innately understood at home, are given little use or value in the external world. In many educational or social situations, our spiritual beliefs are perceived as naïve or inappropriate. We are ridiculed for being too sensitive, for being empathic, for being psychic, for being inclusive, for helping others through kindness via touch, a look, or gentle words. Then a schism evolves within us, as we navigate daily life in a world that is often extremely lacking in love!

The Three Graces and the Seven Sacraments enable us to return to this innate, intrinsic spiritual understanding, and to connect with the Guardian Angels that Diana and I believed in and evoked. Dr, Martin Luther King JR called Angels the 'Cosmic Guardians', and so Diana believed that we each have a Guardian Angel. In earlier times these Guardians were known as Genie and were considered to be the Angelic beings who provided everyone with an amplification of how genius could flow into us from the Cosmos. The Angel's witness allows the expression of our soul's wisdom to be experienced. Diana enlisted the support of her Angels regularly through prayer and meditation, which I will also share with you in support your empowerment process.

Firstly, we will explore the 3G's as golden rules of love at the core of Diana's work, and then we will look at the 7 sage-like sacraments, which were intrinsically interwoven with the evolving nature of Diana's mission.

THE GOLDEN RULE OF LOVE

'Love is the great magnifier of all things wondrous, good and pure, and surely we can see this in every part of creation. Love exists everywhere—from those little sub-atomic particles, into people, planets, universes, galaxies. Countless as those things may be, surely the simplicity of love is the guiding principle. This is what I want to be for the people, what else is there?'

DIANA

The golden rule that became the central axis of Diana's mission was quite simply *'do as you would be done by'*. This axiom graciously requests that we treat each other as we would be treated—with love. It is the simplest, purest, and most glorious maxim of all time, and we are being constantly reminded of this via the work of the Angelic Communion and the leading Spiritual Teachers of today. For these beings give and receive love unconditionally, so that we in turn can feel how they gift us the jewels of their love. Diana reminded us of this by her sheer joy, radiant presence, and immense kindness!

Arising out of this golden axiom are three guardian measures, that give vitality to this chapter, and which enlivened the core beliefs that Diana and I began to honor through the journey of her process. They are:

GENTLENESS, GRATITUDE and GENEROSITY

—held in a crucible that allowed Diana to flow into success, with her astonishing radiance captivating everybody. Diana developed greater confidence through living these graces, and subsequently became more confident about expressing her love, embellished 'initially by'—*how much do you love yourself?*

DIANA'S DISCOVERY OF THE LOVE THAT ANOINTED HER

'It doesn't matter who you love, where you love, why you love, when you love, or how you love; it only matters that you love!'
JOHN LENNON

Most of us awaken to the spiritual quest yearning for love, aching with a deep desire to transform, transmute, or heal the physical and emotional negativities that have caught us in their grip. In this raw state we feel alone, desolate and disassociated, and yet when raw with feeling we actually become most ripe for a sacred initiation. When the world is full of challenge, an epiphany is just around the corner. When we appear to be held in the clutch of an overwhelming force, we are also just on the cusp of experiencing kismet. Then we pivot through 180 degrees, and truly surrender to the loving assistance of the Universe, rather than believing we need to achieve peace through the narcissism of our own being. Through belief, faith and trust in Divine splendor, the Universe always responds, providing us with the kiss of Lady Fortune. All we have to do is ask and be of pure heart!

As Diana showed us, love is with us all the time, right here, right now and always. Love isn't a commodity to acquire. Love is an infinite resource within the Cosmos just waiting to be accessed. Love is the spirit that hovers between the divine and the mortal. Love is the eternal call of the infinite, ripe with the ecstasy of anticipation. Love is the creative potential in all of us, waiting to be made manifest. Love is the very best and most excellent fruit within us, made ripe for expression. Love is the pregnant force within each of us which heals all disharmony back to perfection, for in truth this is who we are!

WHAT MOVES US AWAY FROM THE FORCE OF LOVE

Since the mid seventeenth century and the development of the mechanistic view of the universe, human consciousness has moved away from the realm of the heart in order to favor the head. The heart's way of love is a sacred force within the nature of every living soul, and yet if we live only in head-centered belief systems with the attitude that we can control the world and do whatever we like to the planet, we move away from our core, we disparage our essence, we de-sacralize nature and therefore incarcerate ourselves within the tower of the ego and so our hearts wither.

> 'The intuitive mind is a sacred gift and the rational
> mind is a faithful servant. We have created a society
> that honors the servant and has forgotten the gift.'
> ALBERT EINSTEIN

Our inflated egoic tendencies have led us to believe that the intellect rules, that the Newtonian theory of the planet as a lump of matter hurtling through space exists alone, and that this extraordinary creation called life has no soul. Inevitably, this has fixed our consciousness on the cerebral alone, it has moved us away from the love of Mother Nature within us, within the planet, within all of her creations, and a mighty distrust has been born, a distrust of our feelings which are largely uncontrollable and unquantifiable. We humans have fallen asleep in our heads, fallen that is like the beauty who pricked her finger and froze the entire kingdom whilst under the Witch's curse. This radical shift drew us away from the love that was given to us by the Divine, given in the very moment of creation. A love that has been buried deep inside the flesh of man, the soul that has been hidden for many moons, and is now desiring to be revealed!

THE HOPI STORY OF HUMAN CREATION

*The Great Creator gathered together the whole of
creation, and said:*
*'I want to hide something special from the humans,
until they are ready to find it, this is the soulful concept
of their love, and how they create their own reality!'*
The Eagle said: 'Give it to me, and I will take it to the moon!'
The Creator said: 'No, one day they will go there and find it.'
The Salmon said: 'I will bury it in the deepest part of the ocean.'
The Creator said: 'No, they will go there too!'
*The Buffalo said: 'I will bury it in the middle of the Great
Plains.'*
*The Creator said: 'They will probably cut into the skin of
the earth and find it even there!'*
*Grandmother Mole, who lives in the breast of the Earth,
and has no physical eyes, but sees with spiritual eyes,
said: 'Put it inside them!'*
'It is done!' said the Creator.

DIANA'S HEART PATH

'I knew what my job was; it was to go out and meet the
people and love them all.'
DIANA

The interior landscape of our lives is once more being enlivened, and with it our emotional intelligence is awakening. Diana showed us this. Diana led us to this way, and as feeling is the language of the soul, we are beginning to re-trust the power of love, Diana's love, instead of fixating on the love of power that gambles and exploits the material world. Dr Martin Luther King said: 'Power without love is reckless and abusive. Love without power is sentimental and anemic.'

An arousal of the Divine Feminine is urgently required if we are to cease the wars that rage on our planet; if we are to stop deforestation, and plant more trees which in turn will foster animal life; if we are to love and respect other animal beings many of whom at present are facing extinction; if we are to clean our oceans from plastic bottles; if we are to protect the children from the horrors of the world; if we are to purify the air from stifling noxious gases; if we are to heal our own bodies, and the poisoned corpus of our Governing Systems. And as we do all this, opening to a radical cleansing, Diana invokes us to follow the voice of change as the voice of love, and open to *The Diana Heart Path!*

Diana, I believe, is still teaching us that we are beings of boundless capacity, for love is what we are created from, and love is what we are born with. Love is our authentic nature, and yet like the stars of the night sky, love can be masked by cloud. Then, when the clouds clear, love shines supreme, glimmering forth like the beautiful stars that comprise of her nature. Love transforms all opinions, all prejudices, all fear and hurt, for it is the prime force of the cosmos, existing at the core of all life. Let's lift up our hearts in joy at this prospect, for all we need do is create a loving action, which generates and amplifies a further flow of love. The more love you give, the more love you feel, the more love you will receive.

When was it that you last:

+ opened a door for a senior citizen as they passed through
+ visited a neighbor who may be in need of assistance
+ smiled at someone begging for charity
+ lifted a baby's pushchair up a flight of stairs to help a Mother
+ praised someone who was in need of hearing their excellence
+ gave money to the destitute
+ entered a Hospital asking if you could be of assistance
+ stopped to talk to the children as they passed by
+ smiled and gave blessings to someone less fortunate
+ prayed for the cessation of treachery in the world
+ showed gratitude for someone who may serve you in a restaurant or café or store
+ hugged someone who was less fortunate

DIANA'S LOVE REMINDER FOR GIVING AND RECEIVING

'Every one of us needs to show how much we care for each other, and in the process care for ourselves.'

DIANA

Love like a lotus opens our hearts when we truly appreciate and wholly receive the gifts of life. Of course, we can be closed to love if we are failing to meet our own desires, if we are defensive with reactivity, if we are fearful of what love may do for us, or if we are closed by a fortress of self-denial!

To open the thought-prisons of fear, firstly we need to notice all the riches we have received from life, loved ones, friends, acquaintances, and great work. The joy and abundance received from the rich crop of the world's creativity; the bio-diversity of the planet; the delicate life of flora or fauna; the hurly-burly of nature; the food harvested from the soil of Mother Earth; the joy of one's body meeting the hug of a loved one; the warmth of a shower whilst cleansing your body; the comfort of clean clothes, warm towels and newly laundered sheets; the ease of the temperature controlled space in which your life is lived; the kind gesture of a helper when all else appears unsound. All of these pleasures allow our hearts to expand and grow in the most natural of ways. Thus, we experience and receive love through compassion, kindness, patience, mercy, sincerity, peace, joy, forgiveness, gratitude and intimacy.

Just as we enjoy receiving, so we must take delight in giving love: seeing the face of a child light up with innocent pleasure as we play together; feeling the dawning of inspiration in the mind of a colleague you have stimulated; witnessing the eureka moment of surprise on your own face when a new idea dawns after a time of interminable searching; observing the relief of a street-person smiling at the blessing of your help; knowing the joy of a friend or lover in bliss with the ingenuity of your gift making.

For all these blessings we give thanks, they make the other ugly moments of controversy and challenge more tolerable. Life becomes more precious when we ache for a moment of meeting our heart's longing, after the travail has hit and we have been shipwrecked by life's hurricanes, but then surface to new hope. Diana believed that love was the lodestone of our lives, for love transmutes the deep furrows where ancient hatreds can be translated into future gifts.

THE JEWEL OF UNCONDITIONAL LOVE

'Carry out a random act of kindness, with no
expectation of reward, safe in the knowledge that
one day someone might do the same for you.'
DIANA

When loving is true, its essence is defined by wings of grace. Yet, when tokens of esteem are expected in return for a gift of love, love is tainted. Conditional loving always ends up appearing trite, for it always tries to poison the beauty of unconditional love, trifling true passion. Then when gifts are given freely the Angels sing beautiful songs, with uplifted heartfelt praise, and everything changes for the greatest light to shine!

Unconditional love isn't just perceived with our physical ears or eyes, but through our metaphysical awareness, through the radar of our feelings. Love which pours from the heart is of a hallowed nature—Christians see this as the action of the Holy Spirit, Jews feel this makes a person a Mensch, Hindus and Buddhists see this as being touched by Shakti, Islam sees this as being made holy by Allah, and the Human Potential Movement feels this is an expression of the Higher Self at work—whatever the vision, love pours from the intuitive store of our hearts, clear as crystal, and as ancient as the stars—a special gem of the infinite that always resides in the secret chamber of our hearts.

THE CARDINAL KEYS TO LOVE

'I just feel that if we could all be more caring, more sharing,
and not be frightened to open our hearts, the world would
be a much better place. My equation is SHARING = CARING.
This is my simple truth, and I love seeing the effect this has
on the people I work with or visit!'
DIANA

Diana like the Angels, learned to love for the sake of love, which became her core action. It was rare that a week would pass by without her visiting a Hospital to give touch, care and succor to someone. Often several times a week Diana would be engaged thus, unless preoccupied by more formal activities.

Once, Diana drove through the night with her Personal Protection Officer to the bedside of a dear friend, Adrian Ward Jackson, as he lay in the grip of death, fighting AIDS. Diana drove 550 miles to be at his bedside, to support him as he breathed his last breath. Yet, Adrian hovered between life and death for the next two days, and Diana returned to his bedside sometimes twice a day. Adrian's death had a profound effect on the Princess, and subsequently she dedicated her 'AIDS Crusade' to the memory of this close friend.

This core quality of Diana's love—compassion—brought forth a unique brilliance which was a sacrament in itself. Derived from this essential belief was an exercise that Diana and I engaged in, as she decided upon the principles that could be used to actively shape her love in the world. It is true to say that the Andrew Morton book and the Martin Bashir TV program forged her connection with millions, and yet Diana wanted to create a greater connection, to design a true legacy for the powerful love she had discovered within, and to manage her sometimes unruly feelings.

THE THREE GUARDIAN GRACES

*'Gentleness, Gratitude, and Generosity are not the
exclusive possessions of one religion or determining
philosophy, they are universal wisdom!'*
GANDHI

The following sacred guidelines that Diana used will help you enormously to identify with her, and to become at one with her spirit. These gracious guidelines function as rituals of intention. They are highly potent ways of living a more empowered, abundant, joyous, healthy, loving, free, playful, and hallowed existence. Furthermore, these guidelines have been with us for centuries, having fermented through time immemorial into these three major precepts, for they arise from the ancient wisdom traditions of our people.

When we have completed the definition Diana used, you will see that they comprise of three verities that pour the love of the Cosmos into your soul. These principles are initiations, they have the power to heal, transform, and inspire, bringing a truer comprehension of who we really are, and what we can do to manage emotional chaos.

The three G's as Diana called them are codes into the core vibration of love within your being. They literally direct our souls. Each one essentially springs from the spiritual traditions that make us soar. Therefore, they are at the center of today's leading-edge Human Potential movement. They are skilful notions that foster our mind, body, and soul, and the extraordinary thing is they are shared by the spiritual lineage of all cultures on our planet!

1

GENTLENESS

Imagine Diana is speaking directly to you as you process
these statements:

+ are you gentle to yourself, before you show kindness to others?
+ are you caring, kind and compassionate?
+ are you engaged in charity whilst moving through life?
+ are you generous to passing strangers?
+ are you always patient and humble?
+ are you seeking positivity in all life actions?
+ when do you consciously practice love?
+ when do you feel grace?
+ when do you feel the softness of nature touch you?
+ can you give more generously?
+ can you not worry about what people think of you?
+ can you see yourself as a being of infinite creation?

The awareness you will build by asking these simple questions, whichever way they fall in your answers, will affect how you open your heart to unconditional love.

RELEASING SELF-JUDGEMENT WITH GENTLENESS

If you aren't letting your soul be free, are you saying to yourself?

- ✦ I don't love me!
- ✦ I'm a complete failure!
- ✦ They don't like me!
- ✦ I'll never meet anyone I like!
- ✦ I'm so fat!
- ✦ I hate that about me!
- ✦ Why am I so stupid?
- ✦ When is this going to change?
- ✦ What did I do that for?
- ✦ Why am I so without purpose?
- ✦ I'm stupid and they don't understand me!
- ✦ If only I could finish this!

Judging yourself is the route to psychic self-annihilation, whereas non-judgment through gentleness is a pathway to pure love as a transcendent force. When we sit in the presence of divine wisdom, we don't become more complex metaphysical beings, we become simpler. For simplicity and ordinariness are the hallmarks of authenticity. Diana had these qualities aplenty, and if we can simply apply some of her magic to ourselves, by not judging, we experience an illuminated inner world, and a much more lit-up outer world.

When we judge, we strengthen the stronghold of the Ego, we separate ourselves from what matters in other people. When our Ego oppresses us, we move into a deep spiritual amnesia, we become complaining and unkind. When we are unkind, we forget that what we do to others, we do to ourselves. When we complain, we close our hearts and forget that each of us is really intended to be included in the devotion of life's holy communion. Therefore, the Ego becomes rampant, and in the book 'A Course in Miracles' it is stated that the ego is suspicious at least, and vicious at worst. So, you see the ego instigates chaos, seeking to judge and blame, to always find fault and attack. Whereas the spirit is dedicated to freedom, love and joy. Listening in a deeper fashion to our spirit, allows us to really hear what arises from the wise teacher in the middle of our profound internal dialogue, the deep intuition within. Then, observing our outer expression means we become more present to the repercussions of each feeling state. We are all waking to the fact that unloving thoughts trigger stress hormones that eventually make us ill. Paradoxically our souls are full of love and reflect Source energy. Just ponder for a moment, would you talk to someone you love, a friend or a partner, in the negative way that you often talk to yourself?

Be GENTLE and see your heart as your soul's compass, a sacred coordinate or USB, that once activated will ineluctably change the whole course of your life's direction. The heart is the seat of the soul, and so by living in your heart, all decisions can be made from there. All that is required, as you form the next breath, the next pulse, the next action, is to remember you are surrounded by, and in rapport with your Angelic Guardians. In truth, the natural power of the Universe will always show you the way.

BEGIN A NEW STORY WITH DIANA'S GENTLENESS MEDITATION

✦ Find a place that resonates the 'sacred' this could be in nature near a beautiful tree or gentle brook, in your own home by your Altar, or at a famous site of worship or pilgrimage, like an Earth Energy Center. Each of these places will vibrate 'transformation', for when we place our intention into a Sacred Altar we are always 'altered'

✦ Align your body, whether you are seated, or standing, and breathe the atmosphere into your being. Try not to use pressure as you breathe, just simply allow your breath to exhale, and when you feel the need to breath, let the force of pranayama fill your lungs and upper abdomen, imagining this force from the natural world to be a beautiful color filling your body. Please do this three times.

✦ Notice how your body becomes relaxed and in awe of the simplicity of what you have just done

✦ Try this three times, noticing your body become more and more relaxed, then on the fourth breath sound a HUM in your heart Chakra

✦ Feel the resonance of this gentle sound vibrating in your breast three times

✦ Then PAUSE and simply hover in the wondrous space, feeling the silence of gentleness reverberating through your whole interior and energy field

✦ Be aware of yourself soaking in stillness, there is a presence there—this is the vibration of your soul—for you've just sounded your signature sound, your personal note or the song of your soul

✦ Now try breathing in light force, and sounding AH or the OM on the dynamic of each breath

✦ Then PAUSE and you will feel an even greater resonance in the silence moving through your interior—this will amplify the feeling that you are now once more in touch with Source Energy

✦ Say through your note in your heart: 'I am gentle, I am gentle, all is secure, and I'm in absolute connection with my core vibration!'

✦ Say this three times and then pause

✦ You will feel a sense of bliss moving through you, and therefore please notice how GENTLE you are.

✦ Feel the Angelic Guardians drawing light into your body, and energy field, allowing you to sense that they are full of Gentleness

✦ Then pause, and rest in this wonder . . . .

✦ NAMASTE

2

GRATITUDE

Imagine Diana is speaking directly to you as you process the following:

GRATITUDE MEANS FEELING 'DELIGHT' move through your whole being, as you give thanks for the token of your existence, knowing that the Universe is a personal love letter written by the Divine just for you!

Are you feeling the wonders that you already have in your life, your family, friends, lovers, your work, purpose, projects, your body, feelings, and soul? These are the vital aspects of life, and they can take you from the depths of doom, to the heights of glory in any given moment. Review your life right now and feel GRATITUDE, even if life looks like a warzone, there must be something, somewhere that draws you to thanks—even if it's simply reading these words which Diana was also once comforted by!

Anyone anywhere can feel gratitude moving through their hearts. Yet how many of us allow this beautiful energy to percolate through the entirety of our days? Those who do tend to be happier, more buoyant, more forgiving, more pliable—and therefore more generous to other people. Those who do this have 'feel good' hormones called endorphins, zooming through their biochemistry—chemicals such as serotonin, oxytocin, and dopamine, these are the hormones that give life such great feelings!

Try opening your heart by asking yourself:

+ Am I thankful for the wonders of grace I experience in my love?
+ Am I finding ways of becoming a greater lover in each day?
+ Am I governing my thoughts concerning negativity?
+ Am I seeking ways of becoming more compassionate to others?
+ Am I transforming disharmony into harmony?
+ Am I rewarding others as they speak of their triumphs in life?
+ Am I determining how to be more charitable each day?
+ Am I constantly praising the actions of my life?
+ Am I seeing the beauty of nature in every day?
+ Am I rejoicing about the natural world by seeing innocence?
+ Am I resourcing life from the wonder of spirit?
+ Am I in belief of the infinity of my soul?

Vibrating thus means we truly see the face of the Angels, for gratitude magnetizes all good things to us, and what could be more beautiful than the Angels? Gratitude opens a pure conduit between our ordinary humanness, and our celestial-ness, thus the local awareness of self transforms into the non-local sense of our eternal being. What emerges is a magnificent slipstream of energy straight from infinity.

Eternity or the Cosmos is a continuously unfolding possibility of pure creative potential, directly pulsing towards our heart from the heart of the Divine.

DIANA'S GRATITUDE HEART LIST

1. I am so grateful for my two beautiful boys
2. I am so grateful for the good health that I'm blessed with
3. I am so grateful for the love I receive from my family & friends
4. I am so grateful for the loyal support I receive from my staff
5. I am so grateful for the wonderful opportunities that arise for me to use my gifts
6. I am so grateful for the generosity and kindness from people everywhere
7. I am so grateful for the love and joy I feel
8. I am so grateful for the charitable work I do
9. I am so grateful for the wonderful people I meet who are so kind to me
10. I am so grateful for the boundless healing I feel pouring through me
11. I am so grateful for being in such a rare position of influence
12. I am so grateful for the opportunity to travel the world and see beauty everywhere

Whenever Diana felt 'down' she automatically used the above affirmations, indeed sometimes using them as she was driven to a formal occasion, in which she was expected to shine radiantly. The work toned her presence, brought peace to her center, and allowed her to feel her soul arising from a fount of love and joy.

Using the following daily meditation meant that Diana felt an emotional resonance generating outwards from her heart, and through the breath of gratitude it created an electro-magnetic energy field, that was far greater than anything she had experienced hitherto.

Through the science of HEARTMATH we know that the heart has an energy field five thousand times greater than the brain, and so when the heart sends out a pulse of love or joy this expands our Aura to the most amazing degree. A similar expansion takes place within the whole of our body, and just as this occurs, endorphins are released to amplify your body's vitality, literally filling us with the delightful spirit of the divine.

The World and the Cosmos expand or contract with the levels of our delight, love and appreciation. We all have known people who have very little material possessions in their life, and yet smile beneficently much of the time. Think of a ray of sunshine brightening the laugh of the infant, two young lovers kissing, or an artist receiving the acclaim of the audience—these are the people that feel intoxicated with gratitude.

ALIGNING WITH THE ANGELIC

'I no longer want to live someone else's idea of who and what I should be. I'm going to be me, full of gratitude and adventure, just like the Angels!'
DIANA

Diana was just like an Angel, and as we know Angels are from a world of spirit that ultimately sees all that is good, loving, kind, and pure. Angels love for the sake of love, and they know that life on planet Earth has reached a critical mass of unloving. This is why they beseech us in their loving way, to get out of our heads and into our hearts, just as Diana did and still does. They want us to take courage from our spiritual endeavors, and live life from the capacity of complete delight and kindness.

To see an Angel, you must see another's soul, to feel an Angel you must feel another's heart, to hear an angel you must listen to them both. The Angel's promise is, that from this time forth we will learn to know rare degrees of love, honor, respect, and gratitude. Therefore, none of life's challenges need be accomplished alone, for if we feel the Angels, miracles begin. As we sense their divine aid, delight and awe come to trigger the essential purpose of our lives. Then we know we are here to optimize our creativity, full of love and joy, to ultimately spread a sensation of goodness and peace to all other people—pure bliss!

Begin a New Story with Diana's Gratitude Meditation

+ Find a place that resonates a 'sacred' texture, this could be in nature, near a beautiful tree or gentle brook, in your own home by your Altar, or at a famous site of worship or pilgrimage, like an Earth Energy Center. Each of these places will vibrate 'transformation' for when we place our intention on a Sacred Altar we are always altered

+ Align your body, whether you are seated, or standing, and breathe the sacred atmosphere three times into your being. Try not to use pressure as you breathe, just simply allow your breath to exhale, and when you feel the need to breathe, let the force of prana fill your lungs and upper abdomen, imagining this force to be a beautiful color filling your body

+ Notice how your body becomes immediately relaxed and in awe of the simplicity of what you do

+ Try this three times, noticing your body become more and more relaxed, then on the fourth breath sound HUM into your heart Chakra

+ Feel the resonance of this gentle sound vibrating in your breast—do this three times

+ Then PAUSE and simply float in this wondrous space, feeling the silence of gratitude reverberating through your whole interior and energy field

+ Be aware of yourself soaking in essence—this is the vibration of your soul, as you've just sounded your signature sound on a HUM, this was your personal note, the song of your soul
+ Now try breathing in the light force three times, sounding the OM on the dynamic of each breath through your heart
+ Then PAUSE again and you will feel an even greater resonance in the silence moving through your interior—this will amplify the feeling that you are now once more in touch with Source Energy
+ Say in your note, in your heart as gently, but as fully as you can: 'I am all gratitude, I am all gratitude! All is secure, and I am in absolute connection with my core vibration!'
+ Say this three times, and then pause
+ You will feel a sense of bliss moving through you, and so please notice how full of GRATITUDE you feel for the whole of your life. This means the
+ Angels are caressing your Aura, filling your field with their vibrant light
+ Bask in the light of the Angels
+ NAMASTE

3

GENEROSITY

Imagine Diana is speaking directly to you as you live the following feelings and ideas:

BEING IN A STATE OF GRACE means that we are protected, sanctified and directly spoken to by the Divine. Being with grace means we are favored by excellence, particularly in the elegance of movement. Being of grace suggests that charm and refinement are our experience. Being in grace means we are rising to the energy of the divine, beseeching the loving strength of the Angels to appear, and so they refine any darker energy that may be within us.

Living with grace, just as Diana did, means the Angels conspire with us to create a testament of love. For when we register magic and wonder in a life based in love, we dispel the horror of fear, and literally leap from the old emotional dramas that were once our life-script into the glory of freedom. This is why the Angels inspire us to be full of faith concerning our infinite potential. This is how we are sublimely connected with the Universe:

+ Am I as kind as I could be?
+ Am I as forgiving as I can be?
+ Am I self-centred?

+ Am I leaving the trauma of betrayal behind?
+ Am I acquiring emotional intelligence?
+ Am I easy with the experience of anger?
+ Am I alive with grace and charm?
+ Am I easy to surrender?
+ Am I an inspiration to all around me?
+ Am I sourcing my life from God's presence?
+ Am I truly the champion of my life?
+ Am I giving unconditionally to all who cross my path, in grace?

THE GENEROSITY OF FORGIVENESS

'When you are happy you can forgive a great deal'
DIANA

Forgiveness and mercy lie at the core of grace, and so right now measure all the situations that have brought about a perceived betrayal or rejection. Measure when love was thwarted by the breaking of trust, when you felt powerfully mistreated, or unfairly criticized, when you were insultingly slighted by one whom you thought loved you, when you felt your work or behavior were unjustly dismissed, when the gift of your heart was dashed rudely aside, when the person who had responsibility in your life behaved abusively, when someone cruelly wronged the one whom you love—all the myriad experiences of being thwarted. All these are the taskmasters that bring us to account, which force us to proclaim our love be stripped to the very bones of our being, exposed for being truly beautiful and gracious, or sorely blemished and ungracious.

Because Diana felt so wronged by the family into which she was married, she also learned that forgiveness was the powerful crucible out of which divine providence could eventually flow. Therefore, her first objective was to forgive herself—meaning that all personal woundology needed to be transformed. Self-forgiveness means that any behavior smarting of 'victim', ceases; self-forgiveness means that we see ourselves transparently lifted from the bog of delusion, paranoia and self-recrimination; self-forgiveness means we stop blaming, accusing or criticizing others and substantiate our behavior through insight and resolution; self-forgiveness means we stop re-acting to pain by being defensive. Forgiveness, per se, means we've stopped letting the pain fester, and so a miracle is born in the shining nature of new dawn. This is when with grace, we fully recognize that the true point of our existence is to love in order to shine the light of our soul for the benefit of others, for the entire world, and significantly in those places where forgiveness seems blocked.

If we ask the Angels, they will always take the pain away. Learning to become more discerning about grace is crucial—for being more patient in traffic, not losing our temper in meetings when the salience of the point we were making is diminished, not springing to defense as we ride the subway and someone is rude or offensive, loving one's child when they have been outrageous and flagrant in disrespect—these and more are the tasks that bring us to account our GRACE and GENEROSITY!

Deep hurt takes time, patience and courage to accept, then relinquish, then atone, and lastly to heal. In order to plummet the depths of the affliction, in order to fully comprehend the pain, firstly we need to spur the heights of gratitude, gentleness, and grace

REACHING FOR THE HEIGHTS OF GRACE

'Ah but a man's reach should exceed his grasp or what's a heaven for?'
ROBERT BROWNING

When we reach out for help the Angels always hear, and so we fall more gently as we drop into the depths of the despair. The Angels will always provide for us as they did for Diana, with groundbreaking strategies associated with grace, that will allow change in our lives to take place. Their promise is that the application of this information will replace all that has gone before, so that we may feel recalibrated to supplant old paradigms. As a consequence, you will draw new rich seams of creative power towards you. You will feel your life being sourced from a wholly different place of abundance and security. You will feel love and joy as your birthright, not anger and fear.

Wherever you may be, whatever your life reveals, whenever you are challenged, you will find a resolution through the Angel's guidance. For these sacred guidelines are destined to help you transform every emergency, every error, every malfunctional system, whilst you emerge into a wholly different hierarchy of values—into a paradise of your own making.

The deeper your conversation is with these principles the more you will begin a magical enquiry into a new way of shaping your reality. For right at this time, we are all eagerly developing new ways to release ourselves from the old limiting beliefs and conditions that have had the power to bind and control us. Just as Diana found a way of releasing herself from being the prisoner of Windsor. For many years we have felt powerless concerning a certain force within society, over which seemingly we have had no dominion. Now we find we do, just as Diana did!

BEGIN A NEW STORY WITH DIANA'S GENEROSITY MEDITATION

+ Find a place that resonates of a 'sacred' texture —this could be in nature, near a beautiful tree or gentle brook; in your own home by your Altar; or at a famous site of worship or pilgrimage, like an Earth Energy Center Each of these places will vibrate 'transformation', for when we place our intention on a Sacred Altar we are always altered

✦ Align your body, whether you are seated, or standing, and breathe the sacred atmosphere into your being three times. Try not to use pressure as you breathe, just simply allow your breath to exhale, and when you feel the need to breath, let the force of prana fill your lungs and upper abdomen, imagining this force to be a beautiful color filling your body

✦ Notice how your body becomes immediately relaxed and in awe of the simplicity of what you do

✦ Try this three times noticing how your body become more and more relaxed, then on the fourth breath HUM into your heart Chakra

✦ Feel the resonance of this gentle sound vibrating through your breast—do this thrice

✦ Then PAUSE and simply hover in this wondrous space feeling the silence and stillness reverberating through your whole interior and energy field

✦ Be aware of yourself soaking in essence—this is the vibration of your soul, and you've just sounded your signature sound, your personal note, the song of your soul

✦ Now try breathing in light force three times, sounding the OM on the dynamic of each breath through your heart

✦ Then PAUSE and you will feel an even greater resonance in the silence of grace moving through your interior— this will amplify the feeling that you are now once more in touch with Source Energy

✦ Say in your note, in your heart as gently, but as fully as you can: 'I am full of grace, I full of grace, all is secure, and I am in absolute connection with my core vibration!'

+ Say this three times and then pause
+ You will feel a sense of bliss moving through, and so please notice how full of GENEROSITY you feel for the whole of your life.
+ Bask in the light of the Angels, feeling their gratitude for the way you open your life to their glory
+ NAMASTE

THE SEVEN SACRAMENTS OF DIANA'S TRANSFORMATION

DIANA DECIDED UPON THESE SEVEN SACRAMENTS, which we knew to be powerful keys into the collective consciousness of humanity. Just as they helped Diana, now these sacraments could also help you to live a more virtuous path, by loving more truly, more honestly, and more passionately. They are divine keys corresponding with the seven chakras that lighten up the energy field of our bodies. The chakras are the databases for the whole of our energy and exist like bio-computers along the length of the spine. The chakras bring forth the light within the nature of the sacraments, which are often taken for granted, and yet have existed for eternity, reappearing in times of unprecedented change like now. They are like the ringing of sacred bells, or the voices of ancient Monks singing out their love for the Divine, for they help us cleanse and clarify our whole being. These beautiful sacraments allow our love to be expressed in a world that can often be out of love with loving, and Diana specifically used them to acquire her own form of 'anointing' as the Queen of Everybody's Hearts.

The Seven Sacraments are:

✦ SURRENDER THROUGH IMMERSION
✦ AWE THROUGH INITIATION

+ DELIGHT THROUGH COMMUNION
+ ROMANCE THROUGH INVOCATION
+ ANTICIPATION THROUGH PURIFICATION
+ COMPASSION THROUGH ORDINATION
+ ECSTASY THROUGH DEDICATION

Often, we feel limited in our ways of loving and giving, and so I am sharing the principles Diana used as a regular discipline to achieve your own personal miracles. As we saw Diana shone so spectacularly for those who felt her, and these sacraments have one essential pre-supposition:

> 'You are loved, and your purpose is to love. Live a life
> filled with infinite love and you will come to a power
> that will create infinite possibility. The significance of
> this is greater than you think, for feeling pure love means
> you will reflect and attract all the love in the world. This
> form of thinking and feeling is called enlightenment—
> but enlightenment is not a process we work towards, it's
> a choice made available to us in each holy instant.'
> MARIANNE WILLIAMSON

1

THE SACRAMENT OF IMMERSION INTO YOUR SOUL CREATES A WAY TO 'SURRENDER'

Imagine Diana speaking these thoughts to you, and feel how she personalizes them for you:

'Look at everyone, look at every living being through the eyes of the soul, and then you will find love and compassion for all. But this isn't about being holier than thou, its often important to have a good laugh, to release pressure, and to turn back to grace!'

DIANA

THE SACRAMENT OF IMMERSION means to totally surrender the idea of the personal self, that part we know as ME or the ego, to the soul of the Divine. As soon as we let go of that sense of the ME that controls our lives, we embark on a new way of loving, opening to the embrace of the WE, and we subsequently cascade into the flow of the Universe. In turn, this immerses us in the acknowledgement of our membership within the whole of mankind, and beyond to the life of the Cosmos. You see, every breath, thought, or feeling, is a vibration that affects the living field of the

Cosmos, and being immersed in this knowledge, links human discernment with divine reasoning!

From a literal point of view the sacrament of immersion, and the willingness to surrender, sees us moving back into the power of the collective, the power of flow, and when we live in this harmony, beautiful states of being are contained within—trusting honor, believing loyalty, loving fairly, evolving a sense of moral justice, and growing ethical balance.

From a symbolic point of view, to be fully immersed in this sacrament is to honor one's ancestors, and the broader spiritual family, as this is the larger part of who we are. Maya Angelou once said to me that whenever she made a public appearance she never felt alone, that 50,000 spirit ancestors came with her. I shared this with Diana who loved the connection and used its essence as she stepped into the field of hundreds of flashing cameras, all waiting to either extol her virtues, or desecrate her honor!

When we surrender as Diana did, we discover that the spirit of the universe always has our backs. When we fully yield to the power of the universe our souls sing, recognizing that in truth we are most powerful when in synergy with all sentience. Of course, to the ego surrender means giving up, whereas to the soul surrender means letting go. Therefore, true surrender is releasing our ego to the beauty of love, to the warmth of the flow of the Universe, and so we receive the abundance of the universe. This truth is simple and unparalleled, and Diana intuitively knew this!

✳ THE ANNOINTED ONE ✳

Looking at my life
I see that my only Love
Has been my soul's companion.
From deep inside
My soul cries out:
Do not wait—surrender,
For the sake of love, let go.
And then the Divine looks
On my frail complexion,
And kisses my cheek with innocence,
And I am smothered in blushes.

RUMI

RECOVERING TRUST

'Everyone needs to be valued.
Everyone has the potential to give something back.'
DIANA

Much of our lives can be spent trying to control our uncertain sense of self, largely because we don't feel enough. This was Diana's biggest challenge, just as it may be yours, she felt this pressure very intensely. We believed this occurred because the intuitive, more sensitive side of Diana's being had often not been treasured by the significant others in her life. In essence we all have the potential for sharing Diana's level of sensitivity, it's just that we don't often acknowledge the richness of its presence as she did.

Diana often felt estranged from polite society, due to many factors, but particularly by the events that led to her parent's divorce, when she was very young. Her fear of loss was great, so it took time for her to really trust relationships, to feel secure. What was wonderful was that she found true joy with the friends whom she shared her apartment with in Earls Court, before meeting Prince Charles. Her father had bought her the flat on graduating from High School, and she considered these girls to be true soul mates, simply adoring them, and remaining friends for life.

Like Diana, when we begin to heal, when we begin to surrender to the universe, we wake to our true spiritual power. But ripening for surrender takes time and discipline, to believe that love can heal and inextricably turn all our situations around. When we do, we are brought to a new level of sensitivity, and so we immerse ourselves in a deeper level of compassion, hearing the story of our brothers and sisters as the Angels hear them.

Consequently, when our hearts are open to this frequency we are drawn to a deeper level of compassion—the power of unconditional love—and so we see the similarities and parallels of our mutual experience through all our fears and sorrows, wants and needs, desires and expectations, whilst they are transformed through abundance. This is when we truly trust, and this is when we turn to true service, immersed in true belief and resilient faith!

Using the attitudinal muscle of surrender means we literally see life through a different lens, and through this lens we develop a much fuller appreciation of our fellow brothers and sisters. Even though we can still see their mistakes and misbehavior as inappropriate and inaccurate, we know their souls are really yearning to get back to the core sense of love, surrendering to the deeper caress of the Divine, and so compassion fills our being.

EMBRACING THE DIVINE FEMININE

'A mother's arms are more comforting than anyone else's.'
DIANA

The embrace of the Divine Feminine can be witnessed in the intimate relationships we have with our own Mothers, or through other significant women who position themselves in our lives as surrogate Mothers. These wonderful women help us feel a way of folding into the abundance of the universe, surrendering our needs to the magical and miraculous intelligence of the Cosmos through their love, and then we hear the Divine Mother's song.

Our Mothers stimulate this within us through the first Chakra experience, activating a sense of identity through their unconditional love. Therefore, we learn how to shape that sense of self, the ego, ceasing to think of ourselves as exclusive, and turning instead to the inclusive love of our fellows. Needless to say, it's very difficult to do this with a heart full of anger, bitterness, disappointment, or hatred.

If, for some reason our Mothers are absent, or have moved from their instinctual path in caring for us, we can always turn to the Divine Mother—to Mary, Isis, Quan Yin, Fatimah, or Devi Shakti. The Prophet writes in the Quran that: 'to bow at the feet of the Sacred Mother is to know the touch of paradise!'

My own mother died many years ago, and I wouldn't feel centered in my being, or practice my core beliefs, if I didn't once a week attend to the ritual of visiting my Sacred Mother—to thank her for her beautiful love and care. This can be in Church, Temple, or in Nature. Diana also did this when she was alive, and it helped her hugely, as she also felt that her childhood had been estranged from her Mother, and then during her later life she felt distanced from her symbolic Mother, in the form of Queen Elizabeth.

OFFERING MOTHERING TO THOSE WHO ARE IN NEED

'Don't call me an icon.
I'm just a mother trying to help.'
DIANA

When our primary love needs are fulfilled, we feel a ravishing sense of balance within our identity, and the first chakra associated with our basic survival function tunes us to a richer harmony. Comprehending other people's needs before our own, brings awareness that our own conversation with sorrow and desperation can evaporate. Loving becomes so much easier as we transcend the malaise of narcissism and depression—both unfortunate byproducts of our journey towards personal sovereignty—then we become able to embrace and open our hearts to those in need, just as Diana did.

DIANA'S INSPIRATIONAL PRAYER FOR BEING IMMERSED IN SURRENDER & GRATITUDE:

From the God and Goddess of my being, I give thanks for the love that I am, for the love in my life, and all the love that surrounds me, thank you.

Thank you for the miracle of life that I am, which I see reflected in all about me, thank you.

Thank you for the gift of life that I am, thank you.

Thank you for this perfect body that I am, for my health and wellbeing, I say thank you.

Thank you for the abundance that I am, and the abundance I see reflected in all about me, thank you.

Thank you for the richness of my life in the I am, and for the river of abundant money that flows to me, thank you.

Thank you for the excitement and adventure of the millions of wondrous possibilities and probabilities in my I am, thank you.

Thank you for the love, wonderment and joy, thank you.

Thank you for the beauty and harmony, thank you.

Thank you for the peace and tranquility, thank you.

Thank you for the laughter and the play, thank you.

Thank you for the privilege of serving and sharing the gift of what I am.

Thank you! Thank you! Thank you!

2

THE SACRAMENT OF INITIATION CREATES 'AWE'

Imagine Diana speaking these thoughts, as she did to me, and feel how she personalizes them for you:

'I no longer want to live as someone else's idea of who or what I should be. I'm going to be me, and my liberation makes me feel marvelous!'
DIANA

AWE AND JOY MAKE US BREAK OUT of the prison of our own consciousness, for they are the gatekeepers to the mystical pathway. This is the path of pure love, and in this regard, we can all remember the great initiations that shone through the face of Diana, as she experienced her newly found joy. True joy generates from deep within us, and does not depend on what we have, or haven't acquired. Joy and awe are vital for our wellbeing, our beauty, and our sense of wonder—all of which connect us to the Angels as messengers of the Divine.

THE ACTIVISM OF LOVE

'It's easy to believe in love when you're surrounded by kindness. It's not so easy when you are confronted by the judgments and attacks of the world!'
MARIANNE WILLIAMSON

Diana's life was also a way of initiating you into a new way of loving, so that you could love with the pure joy that she did, this was her message and her destiny. Believing in this awesome power of love is wonderful, but the crux of the matter lies in how you choose to love. We are often challenged by living our lives in a system that merely encourages a cerebral interaction with life; we are tested by our nearest and dearest when they are contemptuous; we are challenged by our guilt when we see a street person persistent in their begging; we are outraged by the controlling boss whose demands appear insane—all of these conditions and more make fierce petition of us, they truly measure and stretch our love to its fullest account.

PUTTING LOVE FIRST

'Life's Blueprint has three actions: Firstly, believe in your own worth, your dignity, your essence, for you count.

*Secondly, determine how to be the very best of you, so
that everything you do is done with excellence. Thirdly,
commit to love, beauty and justice in all things.'*
MARTIN LUTHER KING JR

Observing awe and joy through the lens of Diana's eyes, was
to become aware of our divine purpose for being here, by
feeling the joyous love with which she regarded all people.
You are special no matter what, and inspired by this you can
then place your love in reverence for the nature of life as
sacred and magical.

Connecting with love allows us to receive that the
Universe supports us in creating the great and good things
in our lives. Alongside this essential belief the Angels can
allow us to perceive the knowledge that our lives are
interwoven with the fiber of the cosmos as they conduct
miracles on our behalf. Placing love in this context means
that we can feel the universe supporting our beauty, our love,
and our goodness. What follows suit is that all achievements
become filled with a deeper soulful joy appearing as if by
magic.

Placing awe and joy as the foundation stones to our lives
brings the ultimate abundance of the universe. As we give,
so we receive—what you give out, so you reap—for we are
on earth to do as love would have us do, and this joy
replenishes or rewires our spiritual awesomeness so that we
may optimize our creativity. Awe and joy are like the oxygen
that keeps our soul alive, for the soul craves meaning just as
the body craves oxygen.

These energies are largely synthesized by our second Chakra, which is dedicated to the force of our relationships—relationships are core to our existence, and so I refer to the bonds we have with significant others, with social forms within establishment, and with weight, space and time. Rooting ourselves in the security of our relationship with the Divine draws us into the space of wonder, governed by the gatekeepers of awe and joy!

RECLAIMING THE WONDER IN LIFE

The role of 'wonder' in our lives has a special position and significance, for wonder lives in respect of both awe and joy. Wonder enlarges the heart and swells our blood vessels with joy. Consequently, when we truly feel wonder we are drawn into a much larger realm of delight, away from the humdrum of life and into the place of the sacred. Then thought and feeling take leave of their usual pattern of being, regaining their original impulse in reverence of the great mystery of life, and wonder confers the highest dignity upon us, by awakening us to the magic and enchantment of the world.

Wonder never explores a surface situation because it wants to voyage deeply inward and highly upward, discovering essential meaning. Real wonder about our soul demands awareness from the deeper inner folds of creation, where all polarity joins as one. Closing oneself off to wonder, losing a sense of wonder, not believing in wonder, means we lose the sacred majesty of the world, and unfortunately as we know too well, this can often ransack a person's life of its bounty.

A year ago or so, I was asked to present a series of Miracle Workshops and so spent time in quiet contemplation, meditating and listening to the Angels after prayer. I asked: 'What would you have me say? What would you have me do? What would you have me be? What would you have me think, and what would you have me feel?' At that moment an anonymous Face Book post appeared in my newsfeed:

'Do you remember the great freedoms that brimmed from your consciousness when you were a child. You were born with comets, hurricanes, mountains, lakes, thunder, and lightning within you. You were born with the insight to read your destiny in grains of sand, to read the clouds, to see the wind altering the perceptions of your days, and to sing the language of the birds, and of the Angels.

Then, this magic was educated out of your soul—it was inoculated out, churched out, moraled out, knocked out, disdained out, and bullied out—for you were taught the illusion of doing. Then you were told to stop crying, to grow up, to muscle up, to die to your imagination, to stop the visions, and do you know why? The people who told you were afraid of their own feelings, they were fearful of the wildness and the beauty of their hearts. They allowed their own magic to wither, almost to the death of their soul. And so let us pray for their souls!'

ENTHUSIASM

Awe and joy bring us to the enthusiasm of wonder, which tunes us back into the most vital substance of our lives, the essence of our Divinity. Did you know that the word 'enthusiasm' in Greek means: blessed by God's joyous essence? If you seek out wonder and joy wherever you go, just as Diana did, you will see people are changed by your enthusiasm, as they become full of the love that radiates from your being. This is what Diana did, because she truly wanted us to know that the deeper textures of awe and joy pour from our unique relationship with the world through the second chakra, which initiates our desire to relate openly and lovingly.

DIANA'S INSPIRATIONAL PROSE PRAYER FOR BEING INITIATED IN AWE & JOY:

'There is a Sacred Knighthood of our time whose members do not ride through the dark of the forests of old, but instead through the forests of the darkened minds. They are armed with a spiritual armor, and an inner sun makes them radiant. Out of them shines an intense love, a healing that flows from the knowledge of mankind as a joyous collection of spiritual beings. Their

*honorable way creates the awesome light of inner
balance, inner justice, inner conviction, and inner
peace. For they know they move with the Angels.'*
KARL KOENIG

3

🌿

THE SACRAMENT OF COMMUNION
CREATES 'DELIGHT'

Imagine Diana speaking these thoughts, as she did to
me, and feel how she personalizes them for you:

The sacrament of communion radiates through a love of
life, and our life of love. It is the direct currency from the
Divine Matrix. It acknowledges everyone we know as
significant, as being part of our life's design. It exists to
sanctify whom we wish 'to break bread with', and its theme
is a deep appreciation for the essence of the broader spiritual
community, as a vessel through which the purity of love can
flow.

To be delighted is to be lit up by the magic and miracle
of devotion, to be alight with love is to be illuminated by
the power of the Source. When we are delighted, each of the
fifty trillion cells in our body's light up. When we are as

delighted as Diana could be, we became charmed and enchanted by the light of the cosmos shining through us. When we are delighted our bodies experience the love and pleasure of the Angels as Cosmic Guardians. When we are delighted the higher vibration of joy spreads through our being, and our aura lights up like a beacon of abundance. When we are delighted the flow of life takes us into areas of such success, for success is sustainable joy!

Delight was the currency of Diana's love making. Delight was the pure cosmic electricity that lit up Diana's cells with love. Delight is the vibration we experience when the light of the universe, electrified by the divine flows through our flesh. Delight is the universe responding to us because it is wired within our beings, just like the electrical wiring of a building is wired. Our body lights up via the energy flooding through the physical wiring of our meridians and arteries. Therefore, our whole being operates rather like a lamp being switched on. Yet, like all lamps, firstly they need to be plugged in for them to be 'switched on'!

CREATING RIPPLES OF DELIGHT

'Each time a person stands for an ideal, or acts to improve the lot of others, or strikes out at injustice, he or she sends forth ripples of hope. All these ripples move through millions of other energy centers in and beyond their body. These daring ripples build a current that may

sweep down the mightiest walls of oppression and resistance.'
ROBERT KENNEDY

The heart has an energy field five thousand times greater than the energy field of the brain. Each time we are emotionally moved, our heart amplifies the resonance of its feeling. Therefore, delight is a cluster of soul-oriented feelings producing power in our bodies, so much so that 'hormonal highs' like rippling forces generate within our cells, radiate through and out of our body. This is the force that brings the magic of star quality, magnetism, and charisma shimmering outwards from a talented performer.

Diana had this shimmering radiance, for she was alight with the power of love, particularly when she acknowledged her role as an anointed one. Then the miracles began to happen for her, because each time she gave her love, each time she saw challenge through the lens of compassion, she was plugged back into the light. With every act of contrition or pledge of forgiveness she plugged back into the light. With each hatred revoked, we plug back into the light. With every second of belief, faith and trust we plug back into the light. With every apology we make we plug back into the light. With every act of humility, grace and mercy we plug back into the light, and then an angel drops a single tear in heaven!

Being with Diana reminded us that for a long time we had been in search of the light, and once we felt her delight, we were healed, we were made whole, we became at one with her light. For there is no light brighter than the light that shone through Diana, for God placed it there. Delight, pleasure and happiness are all signs that we are accepting God's will, connecting with Diana as an emissary of the Divine. In so doing we fully identify, acknowledge, and consecrate her behavior as a spiritual mentor. For she illuminated not only our heart chakras where we could feel self-knowing, she also lit up our third chakras feeling capacity, the center of our will, through her powerful desire to be heightened love and truth.

DIANA'S PRAYER FOR PURE DELIGHT

Dear Divine and the Angels,
I thank you for the vast ocean of my heart and soul, which
opens me t my feelings, and to the magical widening path
of the limitless power of delight.
I thank you for connecting me to the vectors of flow and
expansion in the delight of my wonderful life and work.
I thank you that my evolving reality is based on the flow of
divine wisdom in every realm of my delightful existence.
I thank you that I feel at home and secure in the
universal flow of delight, and that my unwavering
conviction is tuned to the greatest, and highest truth.
Please light up my meridians with rays of delight.
Please light up my cells with the joy of communion.
Please light up my heart with the delight of love
remembered.
Please light up my soul with everlasting loving delight.
And so it is.......Amen

4

THE SACRAMENT OF INVOCATION CREATES 'ROMANCE'

Imagine Diana speaking these thoughts, as she did to me, and feel how she personalizes them for you:

> *'We are made immortal by a kiss,*
> *by the contemplation of sheer beauty, and vital*
> *romance!*
> RALPH WALDO EMMERSON

TO INVOKE ROMANCE IS TO FEEL both elated and the sense of enigma associated with great love. It is an invocation of something much more than we first conceived it to be. For to invoke romance is to feel love's purest force creating a deep cellular churning inside, followed by a yearning to be reconnected with an ideal of love that hasn't been experienced for some time. You see we often regard romance from a superficial point of view, seeing it merely as a lure of physical desire, whereas the Angels teach that romance is something much more!

Romance is a longing, and every human heart is full of longing. We long to be happy. We long to be in love. We long to have secure relationships. We long to have good jobs. We long to gain greater abundance. We long to be of worth. We long to be meaningful and honest. We long to be able to open our heart to a significant other. We long to discover who we truly are. We long to be free and have purpose. We long to be successful. We long to be special in the lives of those we touch. We long to have a legacy.......and so on and so forth!

To align with INVOCATION is to be alive with a powerful loving desire, kindled by the Heart Chakra which is full of truth and knowing. Diana knew this and this can lead us to an even greater knowing, that in our longing is a sense of belonging—a belonging to all that is rich, and significant, and sacred.

Diana loved this Shakespeare Sonnet 116, which tells of the significance of love:

Let me not to the marriage of true minds
Admit impediments. Love is not love
Which alters when it alteration finds,
Or bends with the remover to remove.
O no! It is an ever-fixed mark
That looks on tempests and is never shaken;
It is the star to every wand'ring bark,
Whose worth's unknown, although his height be taken.
Love's not Time's fool, though rosy lips and cheeks
Within his bending sickles compass come;
Love alters not with his brief hours and weeks,
But bears it out even to the edge of doom.
If this be error and upon me prov'd,
I never writ, nor no man ever lov'd.

Deep down in all of us, in our search to remember eternity, there is the yearning for belonging. Without this sense of belonging—belonging to our loved ones, to a major belief, to the glory of our planetary landscape, and significantly to the eternality of the Divine—we become deeply anxious, bitterly unwell, or emotionally paralyzed—simply because we don't belong. This was the major reason for Diana's distress, for she was effectively longing to belong, and yet had been conditioned to anchor herself through co-dependent personal relationships, so she had forgotten her unique connection with the Divine. Then the love for her husband was destroyed by his infidelity, and she woke up!

Diana's love was intense, and she would cling fearsomely to the lover she took. If her relationship dynamics were in courtship phase and appeared reciprocal, the excitement of the chase made her desire root only into the person. Then when the relationship reached a point of completion through a loss of desire, through betrayal, or by recognizing the inappropriateness of the coupling, she withdrew, and a powerful force of insecurity ensued. This turned Diana's behavior into a frenzy of fear. Yet, as she slowly anchored herself into a deeper sense of belonging to her spiritual quest, she felt she had arrived at her heart's true desire through a feeling of security. The word SECURE in Latin means 'self-cure' and this loving cure alerted the deeper desires in Diana's heart, the desire to be loved for herself, and not just for what she represented.

Opening The Heart To Divine Love

*'Today I found a conviction, and in so doing I found a
direction I've been searching for all these years. The
sisters sang to me on arrival, a deeply spiritual
experience, and I soared to such heights in my
soul. The light shone from within these Nuns, they were
like Angels with such love coming from their eyes, and
their touch was full of warmth. Then I was taken by
Sister Federica to the chapel to pray with the novices
and sisters, where they sang the Lord's Prayer, and
with our shoes off, we prayed together on our knees. The
emotion running through the hospice was so strong
that it had such an effect on me, and I knew that this
was what I had longed for to be part of all of this yet on
a global scale.'*
DIANA

Diana spoke of these moments of ecstasy, because she felt
crystallized into a new way of being by visiting Mother
Teresa. The two women really liked each other, even though
they arose from such different points of the social spectrum.
And through the beauty of this holy-communion Diana felt
the sacred prayers and chants open her Heart Chakra,
connecting her directly with the Divine.

When we are touched by love deeply, when we are caressed
by the love of the Divine, this is the love that reaches deep

into the furthermost chasm of our nature, and there it blossoms in the fertile soil of empathy. Expressing love means we invoke greatness in each other, and then we attempt working daily miracles through the evocation of that love.

When we are loved, our heart rushes forward to embrace this love. It's like we're someone who has been lost for years in a desert, returning parched not just within our mouths, but permeating into the very depth of our bone marrow. Then when we are found, we rejoice wholeheartedly in being found. You see when we are found we discover our true selves, we rediscover our souls, and so rediscover the divine within. This enlightens our life with a new vitality and vigor. This level of romance transfigures the gravity of life, and our soul is made free to dance with joy, to sing from the rooftops. For it has found the only force that truly moves its existence, the meeting point between the love of the lover, and therefore the love of God.

5

THE SACRAMENT OF PURIFICATION CREATES 'ANTICIPATION'

Imagine Diana speaking these thoughts, as she did to me, and feel how she personalizes them for you:

THE SACRAMENT OF PURIFICATION lies within the potential of each moment, in each holy instant, as we anticipate that when we relinquish our creative desire into the hands of Divine Will, we gain a reunion with the purest aspect of our soul.

Anticipation is that gusto of energy that bursts forth in the flow that shivers with realization, just before the future dawns rich with the promise of the infinite. Anticipations are pregnant with specialness, with premonition, with precognition, with intuition. Anticipations are the law of attraction in motion, created by us yet uplifted by the Angels. For anticipations are the glorious rockets of desire that charge our lives into manifestation. Anticipations opaque the crudity of expectation for they never fixate on outcome, and as we give our lives to the Divine, we also surrender our personal will to the Source.

Diana made her ability to make love the bottom and the top line. She took love to the heights of making her love a fun, easy, yet an intent business, suggesting that she was on earth to do as love would have her do—to use her love fully, to the extent that it awakened her internal guidance system, her soul. Diana set into stark relief that some of us possess a fear of love, a fear that if we give ourselves to love we could dissolve into a pool of insecurity, that love would make us more vulnerable to hurt, that love would make us less effective in the world. And in answer, what Diana showed us was that LOVE WAS HER SANITY—that love doesn't ruin things, rather that love makes all things heal into rightness!

RETURNING TO LOVE

The people of the world often career away from 'right mindedness', as a result of their inappropriate choices, and so veer away from love. Look at the way our relationships are marred by callous behaviour, until we return to love. Look at the way that the world is strewn with the horror of greed, war and genocide, until it returns to love. Look at the way Diana dismayed the core aspect of the British establishment, and then pulled back into favour with love. Love makes all things right by aligning mortal events in our personal lives or in the life of the collective, with the natural rhythms of the Universe, which are rich with intention and creativity. Being within these rhythms means we move completely away from 'wrong minded-ness'.

Martin Luther King JR is reported to have said: '*The arc of the moral universe is long, but it always bends towards justice!*' When we turn away from love, we are ultimately always returned back to love, even if it takes time, maybe life times—this is what the Universe does. In each lifetime we have the opportunity to absolve our karma and atone our sins. Similarly, in each new day the Universe will realign us away from transgression and back to impeccability. (Remember impeccable means 'without sin') Except, that is when we interfere with the natural laws of the Universe, and our souls are held in suspension within the law of karma. When the essence and fabric of love is torn, the natural laws of the Universe appear shattered, until cosmic forces restore them to right balance.

'*The moment you are knocked down,*
Is the moment when you may truly frown,
Yet this is the moment that really counts,
For this is when you can create self-account.
This is the moment when you can surrender your personality,
For this is a unique moment of your destiny.
When your eyes are full of tears,
And you are full to the brim with fears,
This is when you need to be brave and stark,
And know that you're only actually fearful of the dark.
Because your whole being loves the light,
You say you're sometimes fearful of the night.
You say you're really scared of heights,

But the only reason you think it, creates this plight,
Because you've been so high with joy before,
And now you're only seeing the view from the floor!'
SOURCE UNKNOWN

A SELF-CORRECTING UNIVERSE

The universe is completely self-correcting and self-organizing, healing itself and us back into the circuitry from which love and peace arise. The world and we also, have an internal circuitry that corrects in the same way, the prime creator made sure of this. For we have within us a powerful inner teacher, a mighty wizard which we know as our intuition, and in the perspective of the Universe this wise tutor is the Holy Spirit, authorized by the Divine to reset any loss, fault, pain, or hatred.

Meditating on our intuition means we can be rebooted by our Guardian Angel, in conjunction with the other Angels and Ministers of Grace. All these miracle workers offer divine intercessions on our behalf to the Divine, which restores us to our life's equilibrium, and brings us back into balance with celestial order. Whenever we need to be lifted above the fixed limitations of the mortal world, all we need do is to anticipate miracles happening by praying directly to these Ministers of Grace. This is something Diana began to do, using her freely opened throat chakra, which fully expressed her connection.

DIANA'S PRAYER

DEAR GUARDIAN ANGEL AND MINISTERS OF GRACE,

May I anticipate......that you will......
Please hold my boys and me in gentleness at this time
through your deep and unending passionate love.
Please allow your sacred ecstasy to inflame our love and
desire, so that new heights of passionate creativity may be
experienced.
Please let us feel your gentle caress, so that we may pledge
ourselves to surrender to your awe-inspiring healing love,
for all time.
Please fill us with your might, as we passionately feel your
compassion, so that we may surrender to the greater delight of
your love.
Please allow us through grace, to rise every day to a
brilliant sunrise and sunset, so that we may marvel in the
glory of the Source.
Please may we bring to all our creative outpourings, the
opportunity to fire in inspiration, so that we may
anticipate the joy that transfixes our love.

We are so grateful for your love......
And So It Is.....AMEN

6

THE SACRAMENT OF ORDINATION CREATE 'COMPASSION'

Imagine Diana speaking these thoughts, as she did to me, and feel how she personalizes them for you:

> *'The planet doesn't need more successful people. The planet needs people full of compassion, so that the peacemakers, healers, change-makers, storytellers, mediators, and lovers of all kinds, heal the world!'*
> HH DALAI LAMA

THE SACRAMENT OF ORDINATION urges us to be authentically conscious in each moment, in each holy instant, so that our love of self becomes a gift to life, a gift to others, a gift to the world. The noun ordination comes from the Latin word ordinare, meaning 'to put in order', and so our love is ordered or positioned to engage in a tryst with the Divine.

What arises from this union is the magic of compassion, as this is the most celebrated feeling that we humans express. The miracle of compassion is thereby the vital slipstream of the Angels force, as they draw the cosmic ray of unconditional love into our midst, to be dispersed in equal measure, through the ether, through our bodies, and through the whole of the planet.

A CALL FOR COMPASSION

'I love because I love, not because I'm conditioned to love, but because I love to bring forth the source of compassion through my loving!'
DIANA

Diana brought us to account compassion in our lives. Diana communicated through all that she did that compassion was an absolute necessity, not a luxury. Diana saw compassion as the force that would free us from our 'emotional prisons', allowing us to become like Angels, to soar above the mortal world, yet still be of the world. Diana's compassion was the energy that identified the vital difference between the mortal being of humanity, and the immortal mind of God. This compassion evokes within us the ability to transit the horrors of life, by giving us the power of faith to see that all darkness can be transcended, so long as we keep visioning the light beyond. Diana's compassion invoked the beauty of empathy and taught us all how we could also hold a space of love and beauty, for those who were sorely troubled. For compassion is how we think and feel with mercy, when the landscape of our lives appears as dark as pitch.

In order to bring compassion into our world, good intentions are not enough, because we must be willing to make compassion a constant force in each aspect of our lives.

We must be willing to breathe compassion into all of our actions. We must be willing to scatter compassion liberally throughout our daily intentions, as though we were living in the mind of God, and with the Angels, as Diana did:

> *'When we live loving kindness and compassion,*
> *we are the first ones to profit from the divine!'*
> RUMI

This call for compassion is a heralding call from the Angels, charging us to evoke change, and so transform our lives. When we truly yield to this call, we perceive ourselves from an immortal perspective—so that when the ego says the world should be different, the immortal mind has already conceived a vision of drawing our soul back into the divine blueprint. This awareness is initiated through compassion, and we comprehend all that is exactly as God intends it to be. Of course, the ego mind loves to defend and attack, whilst the immortal mind allows all to occur; the ego mind loves to become angry and blaming, whilst the immortal mind blesses and gives grace; the ego mind loves to create guilt and shame, whilst the immortal mind lives in innocence and wonder; the ego mind enjoys worrying about disease, whilst the immortal mind considers how miracles can happen; the ego mind spins us into fear about not having enough money, whilst the immortal mind dreams abundantly, creating ways to manifest all that is effortlessly needed.

Transforming Life Challenges With Compassion

Life can sometimes appear as though it's not filled with a paradise of possibilities. For example:

+ what do you do when a lover who has made love generously, suddenly and cruelly tears themselves away from the power of your beauty and love?
+ what do you do when your Mother has Alzheimer's disease, and is incapacitated?
+ what do you do when a cherished child dies of a brutal drug overdose?
+ what do you do when you are suddenly made unemployed?
+ what do you do when your lover is diagnosed with terminal cancer?
+ what do you do when you are involved in a terrible car accident, and lose mobility in both legs?
+ what do you do when a dear one dies?
+ what do you do when a friend is blatant in their disregard of you?
+ what do you do if you are sexually oppressed by an aggressor?
+ what do you do if you are attacked by a mugger?
+ what do you do if your work is creatively moribund and you feel the need to find further employment?
+ what do you do after a child of yours has been cruelly bullied at school?

This list is endless, as we face the odds contained within all our journeys, in a world order that is programmed to be full of diminishment, so that the world appears to be founded on greed, horror and corruption. Until we change it that is!

What we need to do is to start thinking with the universe, from a compassionate viewpoint, and not against it. What we need to do is to start thinking like God and the Angels. What we need to do is to soar into the arms of Diana, through pray and meditation, and ask what she would have us do. What we need is to take our souls seriously, rather than considering them woo-woo or pink fluffy!

DIANA'S PRAYER OF COMPASSION

Diana and I used this prayer as a virtue:
  'Dear God and the Angels,
  Please teach me what you would have me think.
  Please teach me what you would have me feel
  Please teach me what you would have me do.
  Please teach me what you would have me be.
  Please allow the whole of me to be filtered through the
  consciousness of your soul. For I am the vessel for your
  abundant creativity and love, and I know you will heal
  all ill'
  And so it is……Amen'

As soon as we say this prayer aligning ourselves with its full intention, a wave of compassion moves through us, which completely changes its former vibration, and we expand both in longitude and latitude. When this happens, we see differently, and begin to experience an epiphany of visions and ideas that totally reboot our perspective. With this, miracles of compassion flow with a mightier force, bringing courage to repudiate the old worldview of blame and anger, and immediately a healthier perspective of love and freedom is our currency.

This is when the MAGIC occurs because:

+ we meet the Divine Partner heralded by the richness of the past, because now you can prepare for a future that is filled with an even greater love.

+ this is what happens as you hear that your dear Mother has passed peacefully in her sleep releasing herself from the pain prison she was inextricably bound by

+ your child comes to you in meditation, in dreams, or through spirit counsel, asking for forgiveness, and pledging immortal love from their resting place of paradise

+ out of nowhere, you hear of a new form of employment, and one that means so much more than the prior job

+ having received radiation therapy, in allegiance with other complimentary medicinal aids, out of the blue your wife's Oncologist reports she is in full remission

+ after suffering immeasurably from the loss of mobility in not being able to walk, you hear of compensation that

fully allows for the acquisition of prosthetic legs
+ suddenly you hear from a friend that they are willing to loan you money to get you through the challenging period, when a promised contract has evaporated
+ your child is rushed into hospital for emergency surgery, and an Angel Nurse turns up to pledge such succor and love, that your child actually looks pleased to be in hospital
+ you have been retired for a year and your spouse suddenly dies, but then new neighbors arrive, and you strike up a profoundly new relationship with them
+ having had chronic pain for a very long time, you suddenly hear of a new therapy that brings immediate release from the systems
+ your mother-in-law who has been severely challenging suddenly meets an opportunity for a new lease of life by providing charity responses within another community
+ you are deeply in debt, and after a night of despair, you suddenly alight on a completely new way of creating income

All these miracles are changes of perception, and I have personally experienced many of them through my own journey with the Angels. Miracles, as changes of perception always bring illumination, and just like Diana appearing in a room during one of her official visits, the whole room would light up with her grace, beauty and compassion. Through invocation and evocation, through pledging compassionate means to develop a conversation with the Divine, all circumstances change. The alchemy, the prayerful affirmations and chant, the miracle of compassion, they all uplift us beyond the chaos or the torment.

Empathy is the skill set that brings compassion alive. It is the superpower whereby we imagine the quality of another person's experience or suffering. Compassion is the conduit of prayer and chant, which prepares us for the presence of the miraculous. Prayer and Chant affect the space-time continuum and make paradise quiver. You see the Universe has intention also and will not be done with us until we wake to the miraculous nature of this ritual, and see the face of paradise, and find the voice of compassion to express whatever the need is. Thereby we change our lives. Thereby we arrive at that way of being where love, and only love is the reality.

> *'I liked her beautiful compassion, which made her such fun. When I first met her she made me feel completely at ease, because there wasn't a stiffness or awkwardness about Diana, which can be present in other members of the royal family, as they are so preoccupied with protocol. Diana was such fun, and this made her compassion appear like a bright light.'*
> SIR ELTON JOHN

7

🌿

THE SACRAMENT OF DEDICATION CREATES 'ECSTASY'

Imagine Diana speaking these thoughts, as she did to me, and feel how she personalizes them for you:

THE SACRAMENT OF DEDICATION provides us with a gateway to transcendence, and a fuller comprehension of being at one with the great heart of the Universe. For you see the love that we experience through ecstasy ignites the pathway of dedication, devotion and disciple-ship, and as soon as we step onto this path we are taken into a kingdom where love is all there is. Then in brilliance the divine is drawn deeply into our flesh, deeply into our very bones, and if there appears any emotional challenge on our pathway, all we need do is name the pain for atonement, surrender it to the Divine by asking the Angels to cleanse it, and then observe the force being transmuted. Restored you will feel spiritual ecstasy touching you from the top to the toe!

Diana wants us to know that divine ecstasy can come in any moment—as a passionate feeling for an aspect of our spiritual evolution, as an achievement of excellence that we've dreamed of, as a dear friend or lover reminds you that the shimmering nature of you is what you came from heaven to dispatch, or as an aspect of love that is rekindled after facing heart-sickness. As we touch ecstasy our whole being is transfixed by the choice we've made, to dedicate ourselves to the mystical pathway.

Therefore, ecstasy doesn't simply refer to the physical condition of feeling 'high' through orgasm, or other erotic states of being. This ecstasy is the transcendent force that lifts us into the state of spiritual beauty, which is so closely aligned with euphoria:

'When you show your face
even the stones begin to dance with joy.
When you lift your veil
even the wise ones lose themselves in awe.
The reflection of your face turns the blessed water
into a shimmer of silver.
The love on your face softens even the fiercest fire
to a tender glow.
Then, when I see your face,
The Moon, the Sun, and all the floating Stars
acquiesce to your glory.
Even eternity appears dim
in comparison to your beauty.
Your ecstasy touched my soul,
and I saw beyond all limitation.
In your presence Mars, the god of war,
sits peacefully in his rapture of Venus.
Oh, my lover, shine forever in your flame,
your firm bliss is my ecstasy!'

RUMI

And so, the urge towards ecstasy is the anticipated uplift into euphoria—that heightened state of wellbeing that has the power to endure all crises.

THE OPPORTUNITY OF CRISIS

Crisis equals opportunity, and although it takes us to highly stressed states of being, crisis is merely a reminder that we've created it by an over energized urge to do-do-do-do, pushing ourselves through anxiety, and not tuning into the flow of the universe. This indicates a movement away from our trust in the Divine, and when doubt reigns with a lack of belief, our creativity is stunted, our productivity lacks thrill, our hope becomes moribund, and our sense of worth diminishes.

Then, when ecstasy tweaks euphoria, the wonder of it all take us back into peak condition, and the joy hormones, endorphins like serotonin and oxytocin rush ecstatically through our bodies. These energies electrify our being, they make us light up with beauty, they touch and renew our hope and faith, bringing us to a place where the dark history ceases, and the future appears evergreen. With the charge of ecstasy behind us our bodies become younger, our hearts flood with love, and so our vision becomes inspired!

Meister Eckhart suggests: *'Time makes us old, and Eternity makes us young.'*

THE INTIMACY OF ECSTASY

Sexual ecstasy invests the aura of a person with an unexpected intimacy—the glimpse, the touch, the sweet kiss, the slow caress, the anticipated closeness, the wandering eye, the hot breath, all are enough to make our hearts skip a beat. Yet ecstasy provides a longing for the Divine, just as we long for our lovers. When ecstasy touches our souls, each moment holds a luminous presence, and those twinkling glimpses of heaven are filled with a grace that always surprises. This is the light that expands our mind's radar for even greater ecstasy, when we feel the faithful capacity that we will always achieve our heart's longing, because our creative process is enlightened.

> *'My heart is so small*
> *it's almost invisible.*
> *How can You place*
> *such big sorrows within it?'*
> *'Look' God answered,*
> *'your eyes are even smaller,*
> *yet they can behold the whole world.'*
> RUMI

Diana believed so fully in ecstasy, and we have all read the reports of her pursuit of love, when she realized that Charles was no longer her amour. Diana asks that we realize the vast potential of our love through ecstasy. Love asks that we show our love, for love is love, is love, is love. We don't need to even know or like someone to show love, and even if we don't feel particularly loving, we can still show it—the more we trust, the greater the gain; the more we love the greater the gain, the more we receive the greater the reciprocity, for these are the parameters of ecstasy.

Diana's meditation for being at one with her anointing

Diana's willingness to feel the loving elements of Surrender, Awe, Joy, Delight, Romance, Anticipation, Compassion, Empathy and Ecstasy, being collated into a crucible of loving was palpable, and as these lines of Rumi suggest, what she was gleeful about was:

> *'The time has come to turn your heart*
> *Into a temple of fire.*
> *Your essence is gold hidden in the dust,*
> *To reveal its splendor*
> *You need to burn in the fire of love'*

✦ Find yourself in a sacred space, whether this be a natural landscape, or your own personal meditation space

✦ Light a candle, burn some incense, play ambient music, all of which will consecrate the space, and give a flavor of your feelings about the passion of your loving—in turn this will fill the space with pure and heightened intentions

+ Having consecrated the space, breathe into the atmosphere of the space the intention to be in the presence of your loving thoughts, and all the Angels and elements of the Divine Feminine.

+ Align your spine to open the pranic cord, create a mudra placing your thumb and tip of finger together, feel your whole presence vigilant, be you seated or lying down

+ Breathe deeply with the breath-light of the Universe moving through your whole being, particularly see it as a silver light moving through your spine. Then, when you've breathed deeply seven times, sit in silence, solitude and stillness, for this will nourish your soul and prepare you for the rich presence of LOVE

+ Breathe in the light of the essence you feel in the space

+ Pause, rest and notice how your internal, and external space have changed to considerably to accommodate this Love. You will probably feel your energy field has expanded around you, and so sound the OM three times, and notice how the energy expands further

+ As the force intensifies, imagine the beautiful being of Diana standing before you—see her surrounded by an intense Silver Light

+ Rest and listen to the energies emanating from the space

+ Feel the space full of compassion and empathy

+ And as you meditate you will feel the power of the seven sacraments like rays bringing you to a new level of calibration, releasing all unloving thoughts, and bringing you, if you will, to Diana's Angelic love

+ NAMASTE

CONCLUSION

'We need women at all levels, not just at the top, to change the dynamic, to reshape the conversation, to make sure women's voices are heard and heeded, not merely overlooked and ignored.'
SHERYL SANDBERG

THE WORLD NEEDS LOVE

DIANA IS STILL SHINING HER LIGHT within our world, for it is rare for anyone to ignore the content of her character when her name is mentioned, without that is, feeling the molecules part around the utterance of those syllables. Diana provides us with a fresh, inspiring way of becoming at one with her, and her destiny today. For wherever she may be, her destiny continues so that we may become at one with our own destiny, particularly through the journey of THE DIANA HEART PATH.

This path is a superhighway illuminating each and every one of our destinies and allowing us to feel a sense of belonging in a world that is rife with division. This superhighway allows us to feel safe to surrender to love, to Diana's love, in a world where relationships are often deterred by our fixation with cell phones in the first instance, and then with cyberspace in general. This superhighway shines light upon our lives, so that the inner nature of our intuition can be activated to create future-facing behaviors, through which a far greater emotional intelligence is born, a genius based on kindness, human dignity and grace. Yet this will have far greater depth than ever before.

The light that Diana shines forth exudes from the power of her incandescent soulful love, which always placed other people's needs before her own, and with which she discovered her voice was the voice of change, using it with such flourish that she could express all aspects of life in joy and with inspiration. This was the light that shone on all of her past misdemeanors as ways of determining what her true nature was, and how she could become more present in the balance of her powerful endeavor. This force still lives on in all who were touched by her, by all who have invigorated their own lives through her example, and by all who live the quality of love that Diana gave. I personally know this because hundreds of people, particularly the women of the world, contact me regularly suggesting they feel a measure of Diana's love nourishing and brightening their lives. The levels of awe, compassion and ecstasy experienced by these people, often suggests that they feel the sacraments of The Diana

Heart Path uplifting their lives, as she speaks to them directly. If this isn't necessarily happening for you, never fear, it will, as you assimilate the wonderful work of The Diana Heart Path!

Diana so prized these sacraments during the last two years of her life, glorying in their strength, triumphing in the use of the skills that stabilized her forward facing motion, exulting in her voice as she championed the charities and allegiances that she patronized. Her life felt more and more affirmed as a peace ambassador, by what she had discovered, by what she had transformed, and by what she had elicited from the beaming faces of praise before her.

The world needs people with love like Diana. We need people who will shine their intelligence and empathy into the global systems of government and commerce, rather than fixating on the ravening expressions of their own ego. People, who will lead us with a true moral compass that abates the chaos and division we currently see before us.

'Leadership is not a position or a title, it's an action of moral composure set by the character of the person.'
PETE BUTTIGIEG
Presidential Democratic Nominee 2020

Einstein observed that the complex challenges of our world are rarely resolved by using the same strategies that created them. This is an intelligent thought and presupposes that we need a completely different set of strategies, in order to bring about radical change in the world. Change is emergent in each aspect of our lives, and at present change demands that we need a complete revolution of systems management within our Governing bodies. Our current systems are evidently based on a form of democracy that palpably does not function of the people, by the people, for the people—but functions instead for a Corporate Elite.

The reasons for this are numerous, yet our central Governing bodies appear to solely serve the Corporations that exist in the burgeoning global marketplace by fixing vast sums of money for personal gain, and so the rich are getting richer whilst the poor are getting poorer. Similarly, our social systems are quaking under the weight of an old ethos that needs reforming, so that better health-care, social services, education, social crisis operatives, and law enforcement regimes can equitably achieve a standard of excellence that produces a sustainable quality of life for all law-abiding citizens.

It seems to me that the mind driven, head led fixation we possess, in doing, doing, doing, is the strategy that has brought about much of the confusion and chaos. This driving fixation solely relies on the quantitative cerebral aspect of our consciousness, which enraptures the ego, but rarely values the intuition. Whereas, the intuition feels its way forward through sensory awareness, bringing us bravely to review the quality of our lives from the very center of our beings, from the causation of feeling. When we feel, we experience stimuli throughout the whole of our bodies, not just our heads. So, we feel the center of our being, we feel the core of our hearts engaged in the process of living.

The doing, doing, doing process takes us away from the heart, and into the head, producing an imbalance between thought and feeling, so that many of us live out our lives in a major state of imbalance, not knowing our purpose, not being happy with our relationships, not achieving the beauty of goals, and not valuing the richness of our existence, as the ego competes with each person. This dissociates us from truly authentic feeling, it makes us victims to the systems, and the people who manage the varying systems. Therefore, in a very short while we give away our power altogether!

The chief propagator of this system of doing, doing, doing is the western educational model, which aligned with our socialization process, and cultural conditioning, is designed to place us solely in pursuit of the 'ends gained' in any given activity, rather than the valuable experience of journeying through 'the means whereby' acquiring genuine skills as we grow. Therefore, our efforts are merely based on the effects and measures of the extrinsic mental body, rather than on the intrinsic, essential qualities of our feelings and essence. Positive feeling states magnetize unforeseen wonders associated with our individual and collective spirit, they reflect the psyche of the universe. Instead, the mechanistic paradigm judges our proficiency, isn't interested in reviewing compassion, altruism, honesty, empathy, generosity, or love. For this force observes something else, far away from the value of residing in the heart of our creative contribution to the world.

A case in point was observed in my coaching practice a few years ago, when I was asked by one of my CEO clients if I would coach a team of aspiring young managers. These 'millennial people' had been educated at Princeton, Yale, Brown, Harvard, Oxford and Cambridge, and they were presented to me as the crème de la crème of the global talent within the company. When in seminar I asked these young people if they would list the essential characteristics of the neo-paradigm enlightened leader, they suggested: 'Driven, Discriminating, Didactic and Determined!' whereas a few weeks earlier I had requested something similar from of a group of young Actors attending a Master Class in NYC, and their reply was 'Empathic, Inspirational, Aspiring, and Authentic.

THE WORLD NEEDS HEART

'My heart is so small it's almost invisible,
How can You place such big sorrows in it?'
'Look', He answered, 'Your eyes are even smaller,
Yet they behold the whole world!'
RUMI

Living only in or from the head, produces an imbalance that disconnects us from who we truly are. In addition, behaving thus often creates a lessening of feeling, and in equal measure, this doing, doing, doing produces large amounts of stress hormone within our body. These stress hormones were originally intended for the fight-flight instincts, and are designed to protect our lives from an attack, by a sudden release of energy that pumps blood into our muscles, producing quickened strength, rapid sustainability, and an accelerated force to move us away from whatever is threatening us. When engaged in a system which constantly demands that we prove our worth to an unfeeling hierarchy, what is created produces fear arising from the specter of failure, simply in order to make ensure we achieve the end-gains stipulated by our Managers, Teachers, Parents or indeed conditioned personal expectations, is palpably insane. This level of imbalance eventually makes us fearful, and severely unwell!

I recommend an alternative strategy, which is more harmonious and arises from the state of being, being, being—a strategy that puts us back in touch with our inner truth, with the health and wealth of our bodies, the power of our imagination, the essence of our soul, our authenticity and truth, and the sense of our loving self-worth. Living thus, moves us into the heart, and so we respond to the fairer aspects of life such as love, joy, delight, empathy, fun, confidence, compassion, wellbeing, inclusivity, aspiration, expansion, and boundlessness. This freedom, releases endorphins in our bodies that strengthen us, consequently we become healthier, more flexible, more in touch with nature, and more joyous. These endorphins stimulate our desire to give love more generously to others, and so we develop a more complete vision of what success we wish to achieve, and what we wish to do with that success.

The former strategy of doing as we've examined keeps us solely in the head, whereas the latter encourages us into the heart, and as we have seen in bygone civilizations, the heart was and is perceived as the seat of the soul. Prophetically, the most advantageous path that could change the way of the world looks somewhat rather like this: let's find a way of living and relating from the heart, a way of governing and organizing from empathy, a way of manifesting meaningful and creative existence from altruism, a way of developing sacred commerce from pleasure and fairness, a way of expressing the means that help us create and manifest abundantly through joy, a way that creates a vision of ourselves as creatures of excellence and beauty, a way that brings the head and the heart together in glorious synergy. This path will be glorious, and this way creates a balance between both forces—both doing and being. In turn this balance refines the nature of our broad complex world, which contains the nature of our lives with such consequence that we become infinitely more effective as global citizens!

This quality of conversation, this way of gently creating, this brave new world, is The Diana Heart Path, and right now she is inspiring us to live from the heart, to fulfill our desires from and for love, creating better lives. Doing so liberates the conviction of our true sovereignty, and all that is divine within us. This optimal potential means we gently connect with the vision of the essential spiritual practices and sacred teachings that exist within the great wisdom faiths of the world, as well as through the wisdom-keeper traditions of the indigenous tribes, to the common sense principles that Diana lived. When this is so we become instruments of pure love!

When our hearts are closed to love we are not ourselves, we are merely hostages to the Ego. When we function as hosts or hostesses to the Divine, our love, our creativity, our health, our well-being, our empathy, our unfolding, our optimizing, and our purpose—all point in the same direction, focusing us into a peace filled, balanced existence. This purity, this free pulse, this easy breath, this cosmic flow, restores us back to balance and brings love to the sanctity of each moment.

ANCIENT VOICES ARISE

As ancient as the rocks and stones, the language of the heart creates a fusion between the mind and body, a coherence between right and left brain. In turn this produces a knowledge base where thought and feeling are one. The ancient transmission center for human oneness was believed to be a secret chamber within the heart, known to the Aztec, Incan and Mayan cultures as the SHANTE ISHTA—'the single eye of the heart.'

The indigenous peoples of South America, alongside the Native Americans of the north, the Aboriginal peoples of the Antipodes, and the Shaman of the Altai Mountains in Siberia all believe that the heart has a secret chamber, a circle of crystals where the 'sacred' lives within each person. Indeed, it is recorded in the book of Genesis, that in ancient times all people knew this one language, believed in one language, lived this one language, until humanity defied the Divine by building the Tower of Babel. The Bible suggests that by building Babel the people of that time 'made their names to be scored upon heaven', and so divine wisdom responded, by dispersing all nations, separating all people to confound the darkened intention of the egoic mind, and from thence forward the soul became individualized.

The secret chamber of the heart is where the soul attunes to the collective, universal heartbeat, and unites us all through a vast field of intention called consciousness. When we choose to love from the heart, we enter a chamber of creation where all things meet in genesis, the legendary 'gene of Isis'. For it is from the Great Mother Isis, that the formative energy of creation flows, from which all life arises. If only we could follow the example of Isis, taking her song of creation by emulating her love, then singing our own song of love, or speaking truth through the language of the heart. Maybe then we could all become vessels of embodied love. Then ingratitude, judgment, hatred, denial, intolerance, lack of compassion, and the refusal to forgive, would cease. For to be anything other than love would be to be without soul!

Diana showed by her life's service and now her legacy that our power to love is the surrendering of our separate sense of self to the inclusivity of life. This is a divine measure, and when we claim our right to be totally part of life, seeing everyone as a brother and sister, a seismic shift of consciousness occurs. Then we cease being an individual in the sense of recognizing our separateness, and we become part of the life as a universal force.

Reality in this form stimulates extraordinary 'connectivity', and we become inspired by the infinite field of possibility, the knowledge of Divine Love as the fruit of all creative energy. Once we connect with this source force, we exchange our mortal intelligence with that of divine wisdom. Then nothing is the same again, and we embark on a voyage of the miraculous. Time as an agent of infinity then expands, allows miracles to occur, and so our creative action ignites to follow the purest of heart paths. Ancient cultures, such as the Egyptians, believed that living a life of purity prepared the individual for Zep Tepi or Paradise, and so lived accordingly, making pure choices to elevate consciousness!

In the ancient Egyptian death ritual, it was believed that the heart of the deceased was taken by a mythological being known as Anubis (the God of the Dead) into the Halls of Truth, where the heart was placed on the scales of justice. On one side of the scales was placed the heart, whilst on the other was placed the feather of Maat (the Goddess of Truth). If the heart of the deceased outweighed the feather, it was believed that the heart was full of judgment and evil deeds, and so a creature called Ammut would arrive to consume the heart, condemning the deceased to eternal oblivion. However, if the heart was lighter than the feather, the great King God Osiris was informed, and the heart of the deceased travelled into Paradise, into Zep Tepi.

We still have the phrase 'if only my heart was as light as a feather', and the following short Meditation is something Diana and I often engaged in, in order to feel as true, as light, and as pure as a feather.

The Heart & Feather Test

+ Close your eyes and visualize your beautiful heart being weighed on a set of scales in the left tray, and a white feather on the right

+ If they do not feel in balance, and the scales tip in favor of a heavy heart, search your heart, and try to see what it is that creates the heaviness, and what color it is?

+ Once you have identified the reason, you will be able to transmute the karma, or sin, by taking the energy into its altered state—and so deceit becomes honesty, or guilt becomes innocence, or pride becomes humility, then you will atone or confess your wrong going, in order to receive Divine absolution

+ Create lightness in your heart by saying:
'I am full of love!'
'I am full of forgiveness!'
'I am full of joy!'
'I am full of peace!'
'Thank you!'
And notice how your heart becomes brighter, lighter, and how the color changes, so that the scales rebalance

+ Now feel how balanced your heart is, so that feather

light thoughts come to your mind. Think about someone whom you know, and whom you feel challenged by—then notice how the feelings change in your heart

+ Watch the way the scales tip in favor of either the heavy feelings, or the lighter feelings, and notice what healing is created in the balance. It's important that you truly review all feelings, so that you can see what you hold in shadow, and what you hold in account. Then the scales will always shift you

+ Imagine yourself healing all the negatives by breathing in harmony, and breathing out words like: LOVE, PEACE, SERENITY, HARMONY, JOY, FREEDOM, ABUNDANCE and then notice how the scales shift some more

THE HEART'S AUTONOMY

Science reveals that the heart of a fetus begins beating before the brain is formed. This 'auto-rhythm' is established by a self-initiated beat, which precedes conscious thought, and so the idea of the brain's intellectual function as the foremost principle in the creation of human life, is frankly incorrect. The beat of the heart is the elixir that excites the beginning of human consciousness!

The human heart has its own independent nervous system with 40,000 neurons, and there are just as many neurons found in the sub-cortex of the brain. Experimentation at the Fels Institute for Cancer Research and Molecular Biology in Philadelphia during the early 1970's discovered that when the brain sent neural messages to the heart, the heart didn't obey. Instead, the heart sent messages back to the brain, which the brain then surrendered to. Sending messages to our own consciousness is crucial as this is where conviction is borne. Aligning the power of our heart to manage thoughts and feelings brings us to live in the beat of emotional truth. Then moving consciously to the rhythm brings about a transformation that creates a bridge between linear thought and intuitive sensing.

Our collectivized preoccupation with the power of the ego, has legitimatized the advancement of the self, and has prioritized the individual over the greater good. This I believe has arisen from a social movement inspiring the creation of the Republic of the United States in 1776, and the need to move away from the patriarchal core system, once offered by the paradigm of the monarchy. Certainly, through the end of the nineteenth century, via the advent of commercialization, industrialization and capitalization, the citizens of the western world became more prosperous, gaining positions of social power and privilege that had hitherto not been recognized. This social development eschewed the need to pledge fealty or duty to the Crown, and consequently the divine right of Kings effectively ceased, as we see with the diminishing power of the European Royal Households.

Thereby, a new gestalt was born, which favored the individual over the notion of the Master, leading us to the belief that we could become the Master/Mistress of our own destiny, and therefore develop a sense of our own sovereignty.

INVICTUS

Out of the night that covers me,
Black as the pit from pole to pole,
I thank whatever gods may be
For my unconquerable soul.

In the fell clutch of circumstance
I have not winced nor cried aloud.
Under the bludgeoning of chance
My head is bloody, but unbowed.

Beyond this place of wrath and tears
Looms but the Horror of the shade,
And yet the menace of the years
Finds and shall find me unafraid.

It matters not how strait the gate,
How charged with punishments the scroll,
I am the master of my fate,
I am the captain of my soul.
    WILLIAM ERNEST HENLEY

How wonderful that there is this insurgence gathering power today, stimulated by Diana's love, and by our own urging to determine self-reliance, self-empowerment, and self-will. These qualities, as we see in Diana's life, draw us to investigate the richness of our creative potential, stretching us to learn how to love even in the moments when we are most challenged, and determining a new path in our history.

'The world is awakening to a powerful truth:
women and girls are no longer the problem; they are
the solution!'
CHRISTIANE NORTHRUP

This is a light-filled time, where a record number of women have obtained US Senate Seats. Where the first Native American woman has gained entrance to the Senate, the first Islamic woman has been welcomed as the youngest female member, and the first Lesbian Mother has also gained representation. So, there is progress, even though Mr. Trump's extraordinary behavior as the forty-fifth President of the USA, brings forth such division, we also see the light prevail in the ambiguity, and I guess this is his gift to the world.

When we look at the United Nations, which extols the issue of equal rights within its Charter, only 12 women serve out of its 191 elected Heads of State. In the United Kingdom fewer than three out of ten Politicians are women, and there are many more CEOs around the world, whose name is Peter or John, than there are female CEOs. Yet, at the same time change is happening:

1. In London, a Mother posted a serious plea on social media for support of the Syrian Refugee Crisis, and in consequence thousands of people marched

2. In Tehran, a female student moved the World's attention to the continued oppression of women by hunger-striking

3. In Los Angeles, a young Mother's statement about her low-income position was placed on social media, and becoming viral, shifted the consciousness of millions of people

4. In Oslo, a young Pakistani woman won the Nobel Peace Prize, having been shot in the head by the Taliban, protesting that girls must receive education

5. In Kampala, a beautiful Nun created a safe house for women and girls who had been mercilessly trafficked as sex-slaves to men

6. In New York, a 29-year-old Hispanic woman, Alexandria Ocasio-Cortes has been elected to the Senate

7. In Moscow, a forty-five-year-old woman refused to allow the Police to arrest her son, who was known to be LGBTQ

The ever-increasing evolution of our peoples urges us to strive to open our consciousness, for we are held in a tricky balance between the dualities in our minds and hearts, between the ambiguity of light and the dark, the soul and the ego, the hate and the love, the guilt and the innocence, the shame and the acceptance. The ravages of the Ego, suspicious at least and vicious at worst, still often holds sway over the glory of the heart, and Diana's inestimable life now needs to burn more passionately in our hearts, and minds, and souls.

Each one of us has our own part to play. Every one of us has a rich calling, governed by the counsel of the heart. Each one of us has the substantial exercise of opening our hearts to life even in the face of fear and corruption. Each one of us has the ability to lead or follow and support. This could be by making tea, or marching. This could be by running for office or teaching the children. This could be by creating the greatest, strongest vision of yourself, whilst serving the downtrodden, homeless or needy. All is possible, and we have many roles!

Many of us will be moved when we see suffering, feeling the power shifting within us to offer compassion, to cease the disempowerment. Many of us will refuse to succumb to heartlessness and indifference. Many of us will face the scorn of discrimination and injustice, calling it out with strong voices and liberated intent. For no longer are we prepared to believe that our voices will not make change, because in unity they can, and as Diana showed us, they already are, and this they will continue.........

'Leave safety behind. Put your body on the line. Stand
before the people you fear and speak your mind—even if
your voice shakes. Then when you least expect it,
someone may actually listen to what you have to say.'
MAGGIE KUHN

PLEASE GO TO
www.dianathevoiceofchange.com

Here you will discover what THE DIANA HEART PATH can
mean for you, taking your journey into a profound
discovery of how to ascend to another level of richness,
excellence, and authenticity.

with love
Stewart

STEWART PEARCE is a renowned global Voice and Presence Coach
who regularly appears in the media addressing the issues of voice and
persona as powerful expressions of human integrity.
www.stewartpearce.com
www.dianathevoiceofchange.com

COPYRIGHT
All copy within these pages is the sole ownership of Stewart Pearce

CPSIA information can be obtained
at www.ICGtesting.com
Printed in the USA
BVHW041146041121
620786BV00014B/263